(a word to describe me)
(my name)
AF585193

My progress chart

Find the letter to match your completed page. Track the letter and colour the picture.

a b c d

p o n m

q r s 2 t

e
2
f
g
h
i
j
k
l
u
v
w
2
x
z
y

Help each animal find its home.

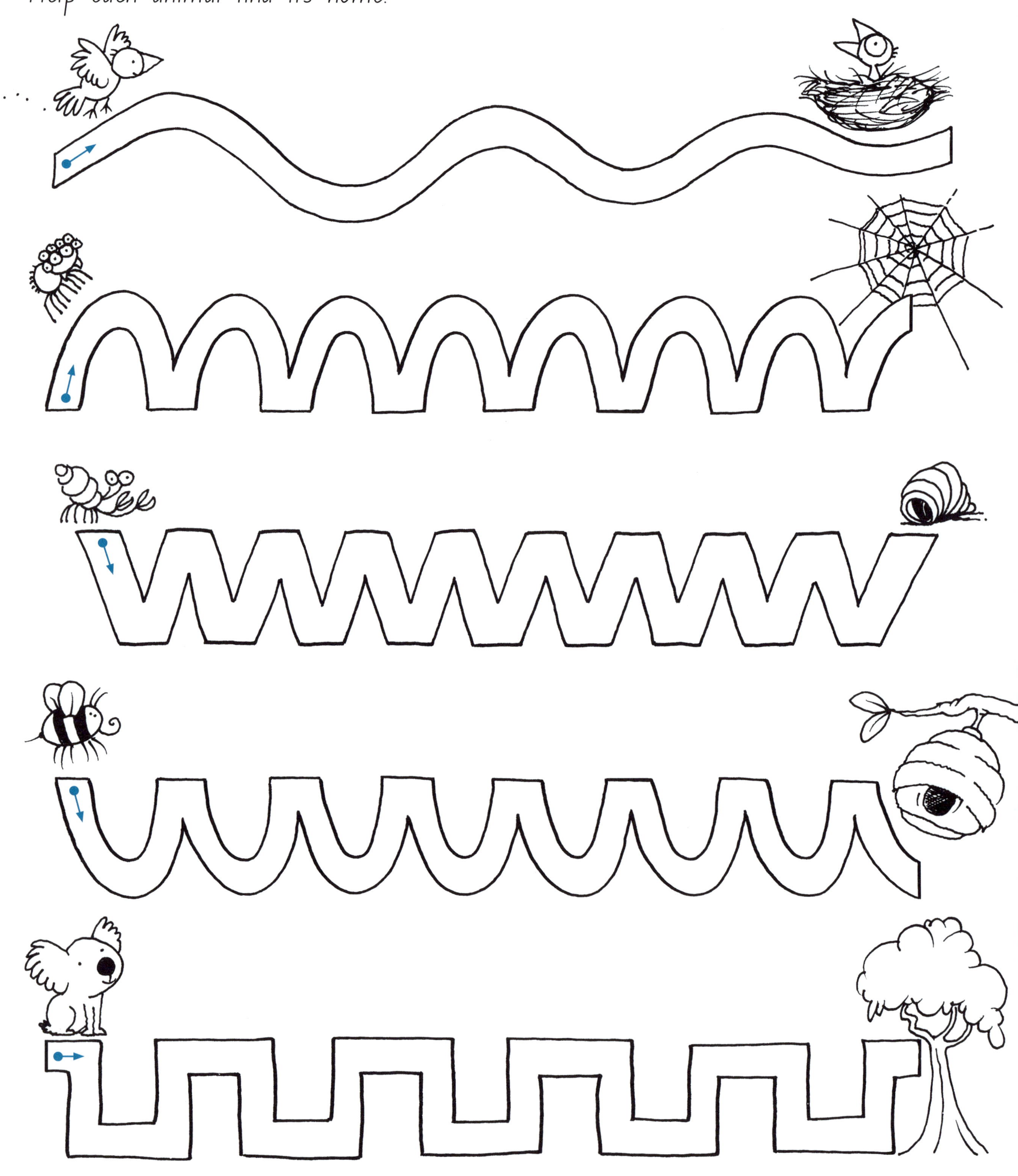

Handwriting: Tracking, left to right direction, fine motor control.

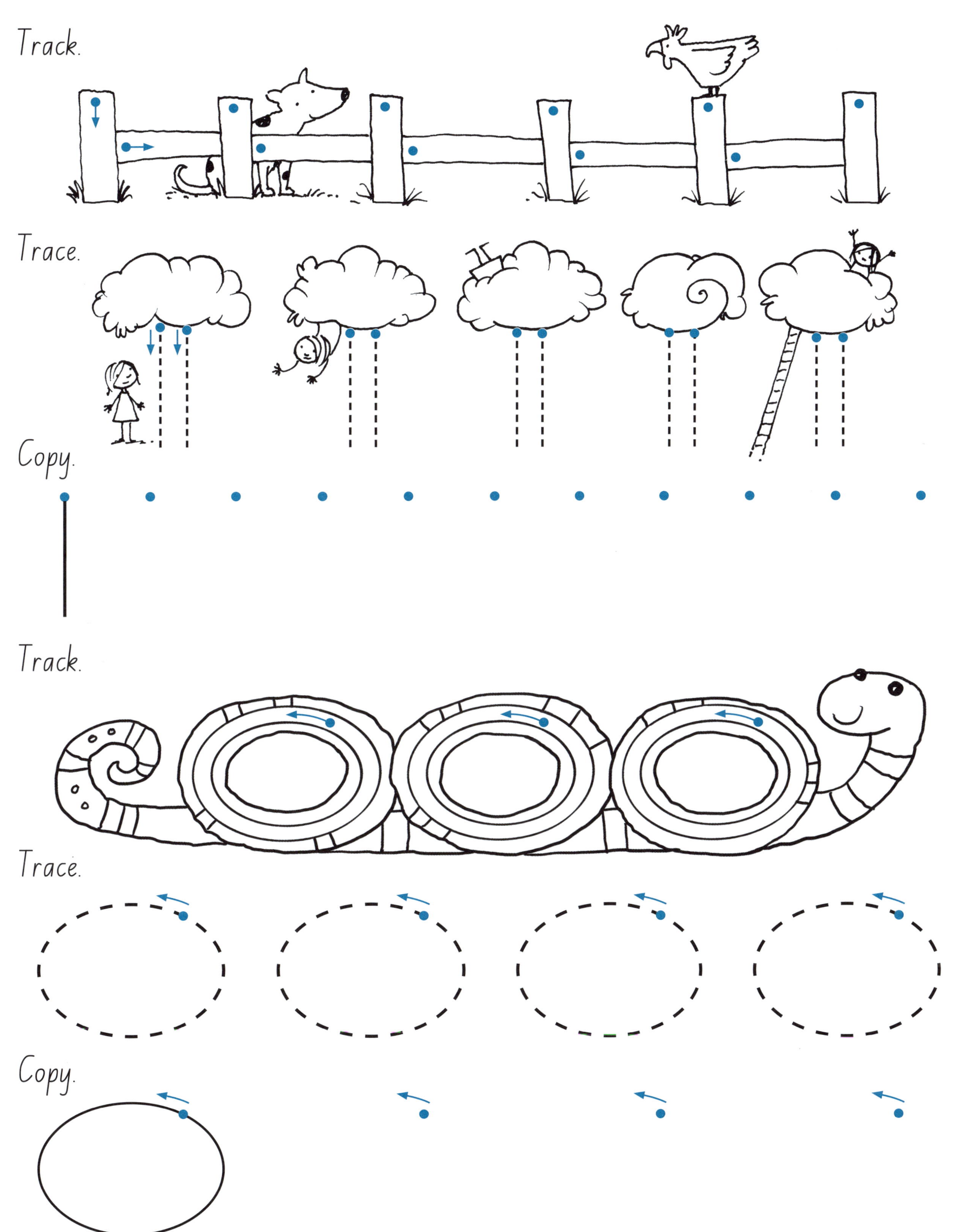

Handwriting: Patterning, left to right direction, fine motor control.

Trace.

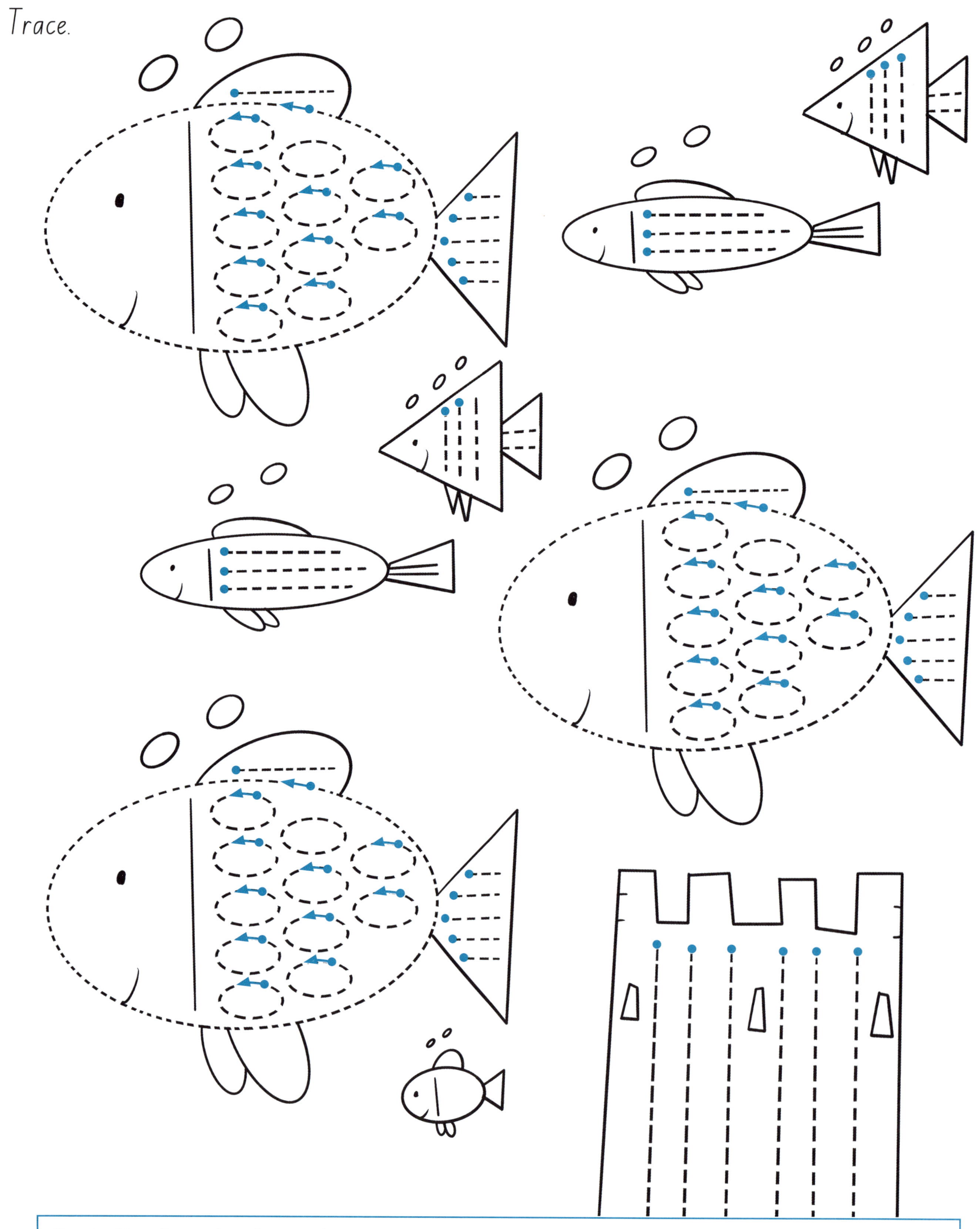

Handwriting: Patterning, downstroke and anticlockwise movements, left to right direction, fine motor control.

Trace.

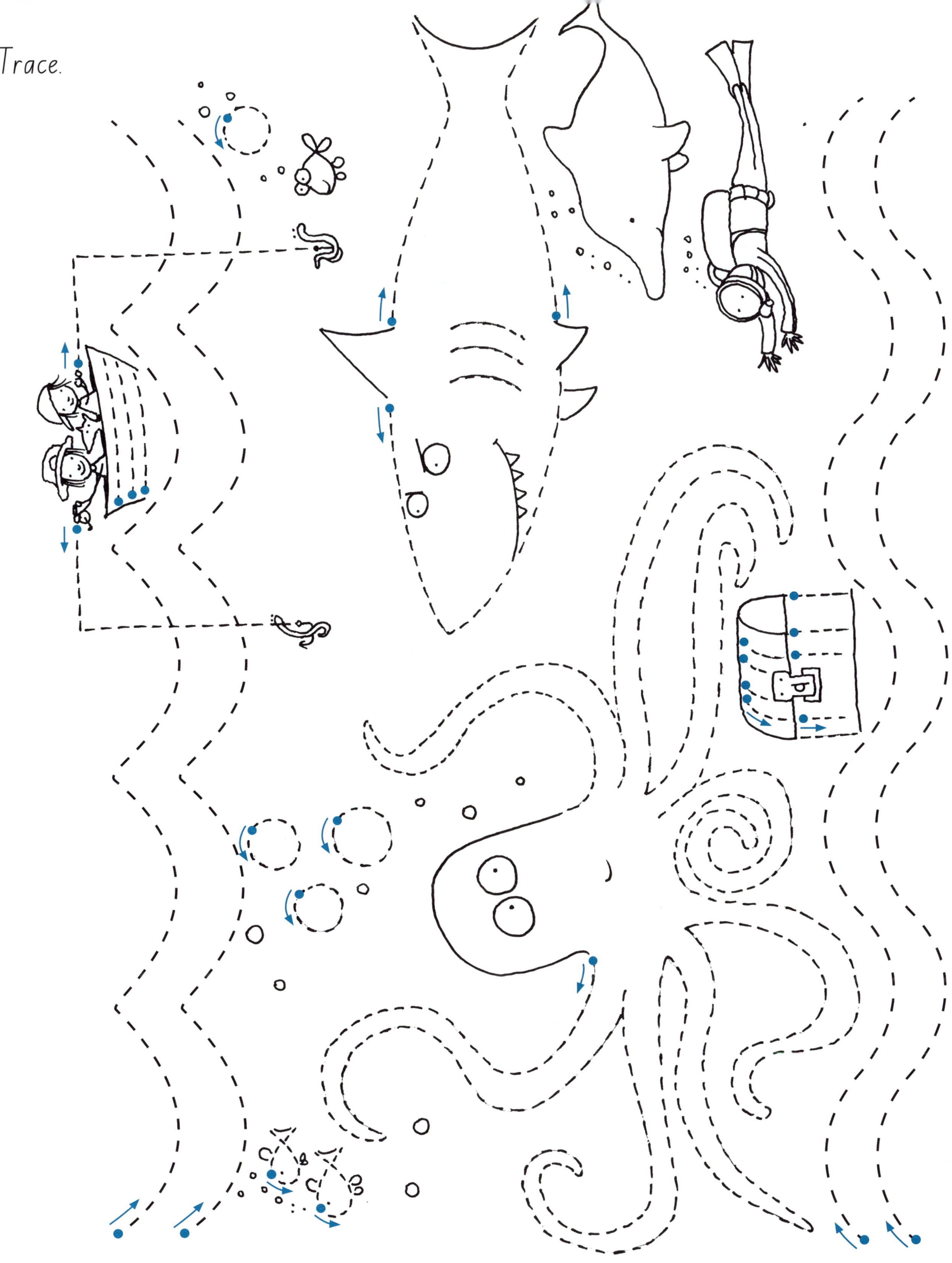

Handwriting: Patterning, downstroke, anticlockwise and clockwise movements, fine motor control.

Phonic knowledge chant

ugly undies

u u u

Trace the pattern.

Find u.

u

Trace the pattern. Keep your pencil on the page.

Track.

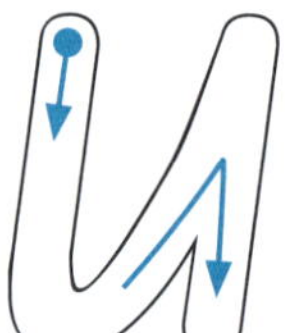    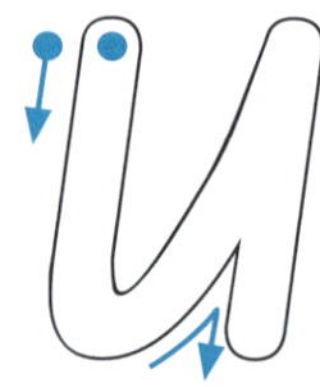 

Handwriting: anticlockwise ellipse, body (short) letter u.
Vocabulary: ugly, undies, umbrella, under, shut.
Phonic knowledge /u/: up, mum, bug, but, mug, cup, duck, sunset.

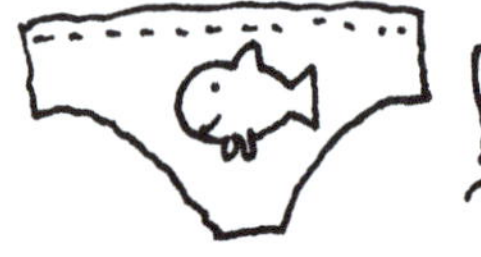 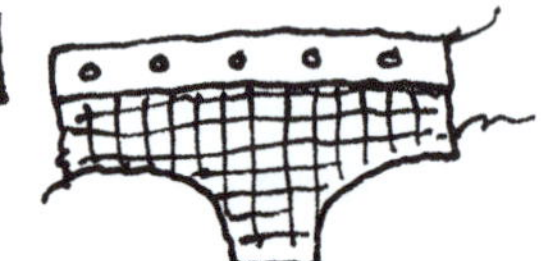

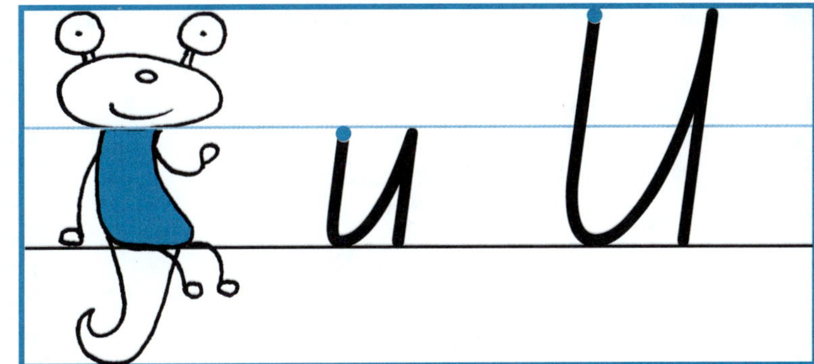

Track.

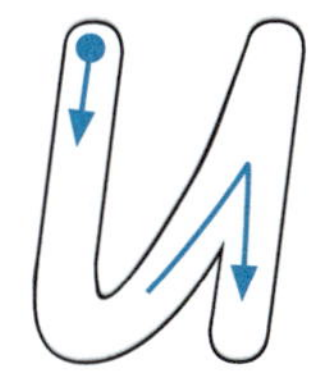

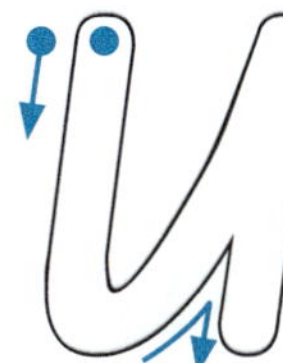

Trace.

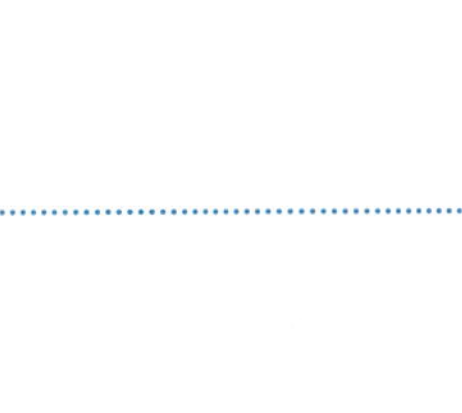

Trace.

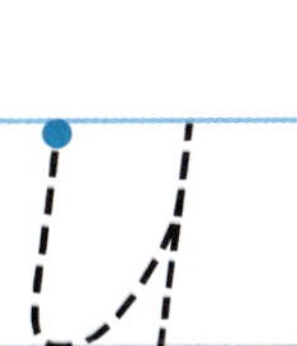

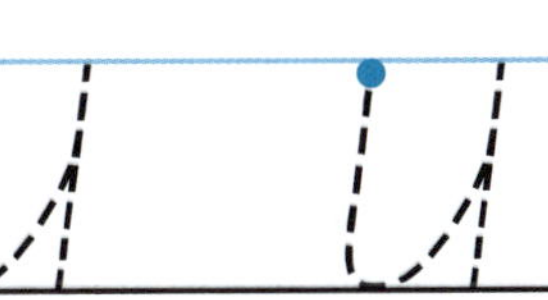

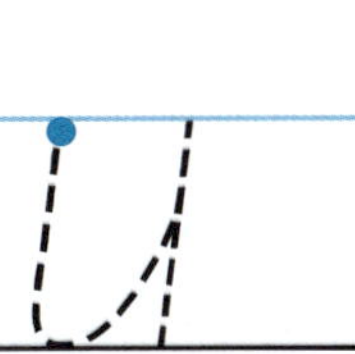

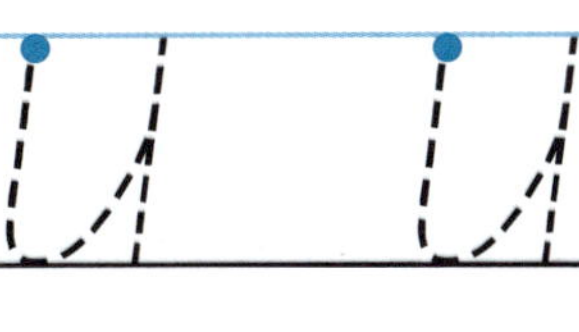

Write.

Patter

Go down, around, up and down. Keep your pencil on the page.

Phonic knowledge chant

yellow yak
y y y

Trace the pattern.

Trace the pattern. Keep your pencil on the page.

Trace the pattern. Turn each pattern into a picture.

Track.

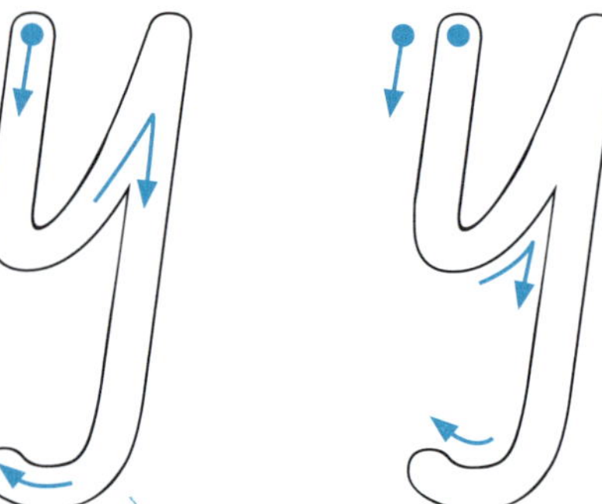

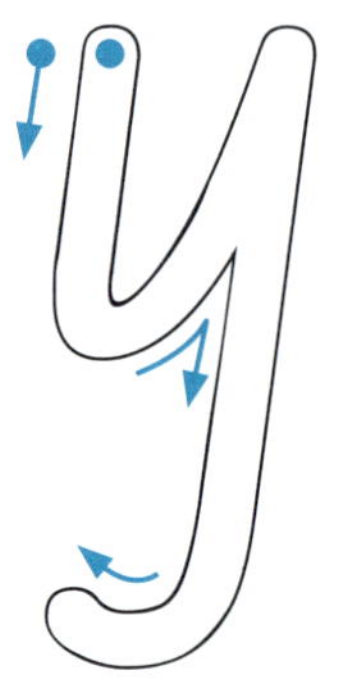

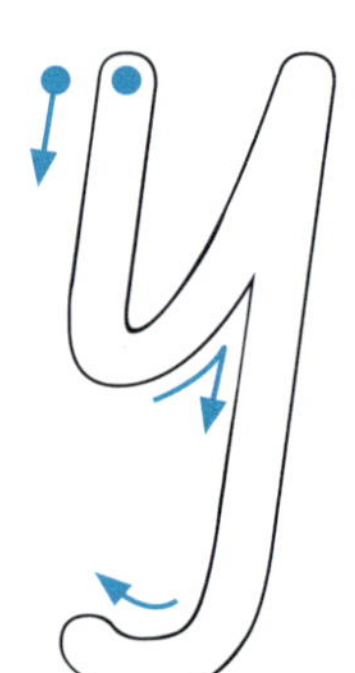

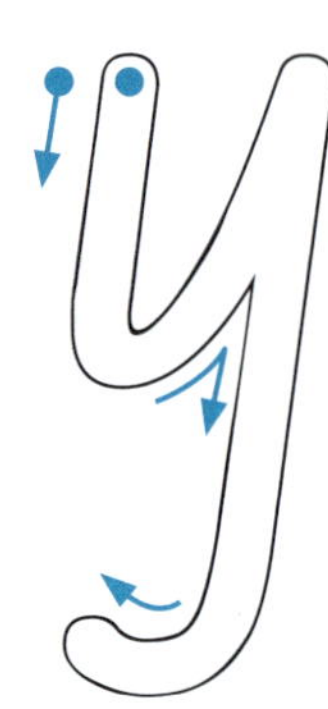

Handwriting: anticlockwise ellipse, body and tail (long) letter y.
Vocabulary: yak, yellow, yo-yo.
Phonic knowledge /y/: yell, yes, yet, yap, yum.

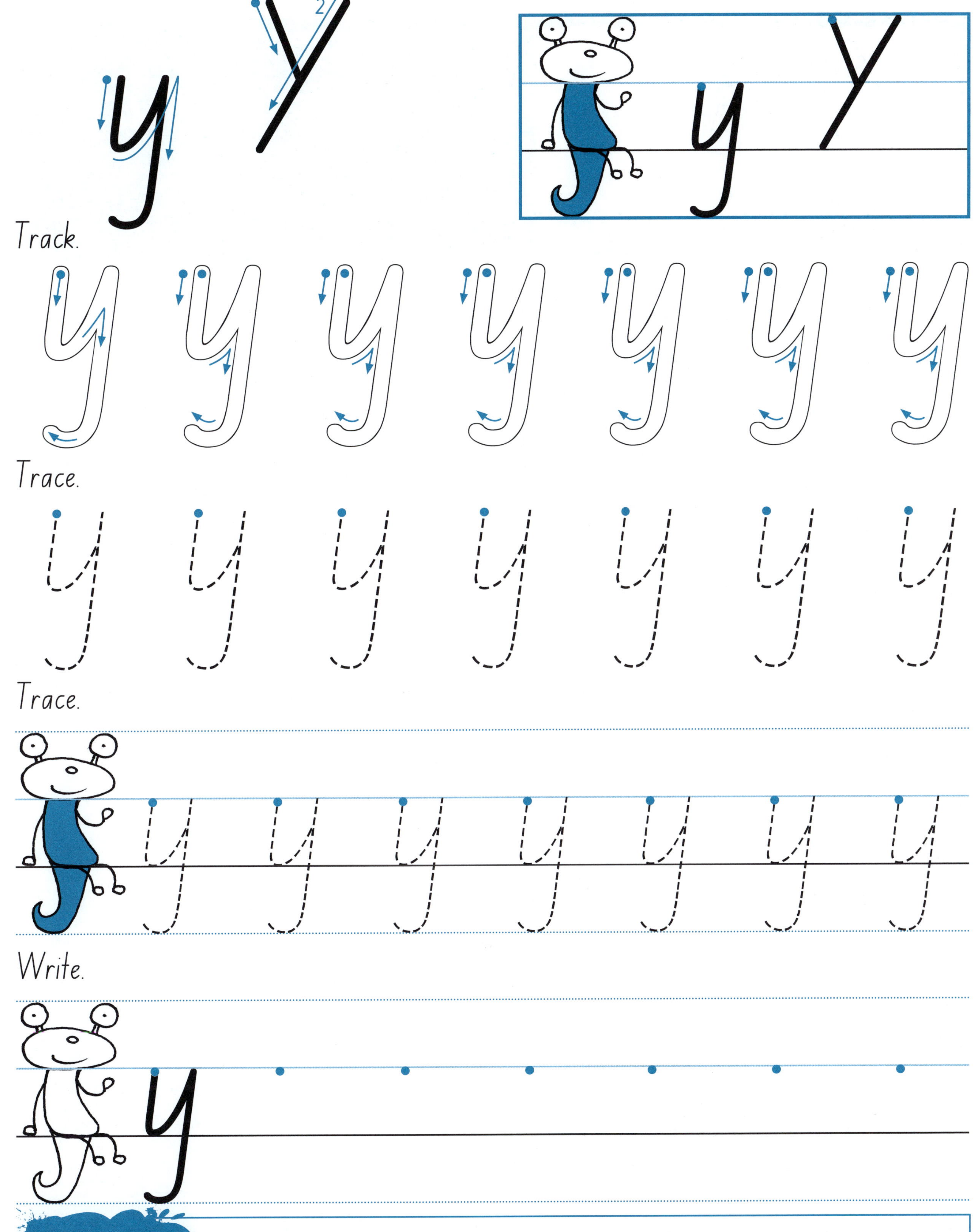

Go down, around, up and down to make a tail. Keep your pencil on the page.

Phonic knowledge chant

vicious vulture

v v v

Trace the pattern.

Trace the pattern. Keep your pencil on the page.

Trace the pattern. Turn each pattern into a picture.

Track.

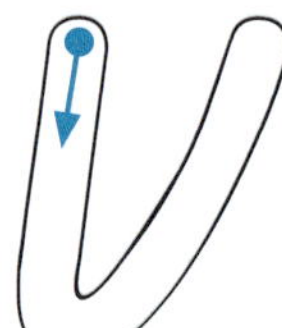

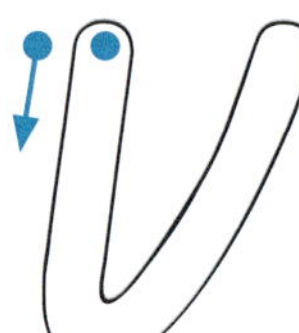

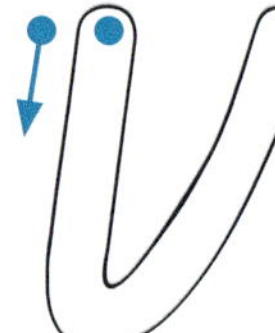

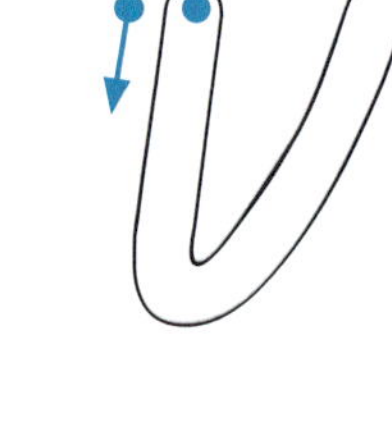

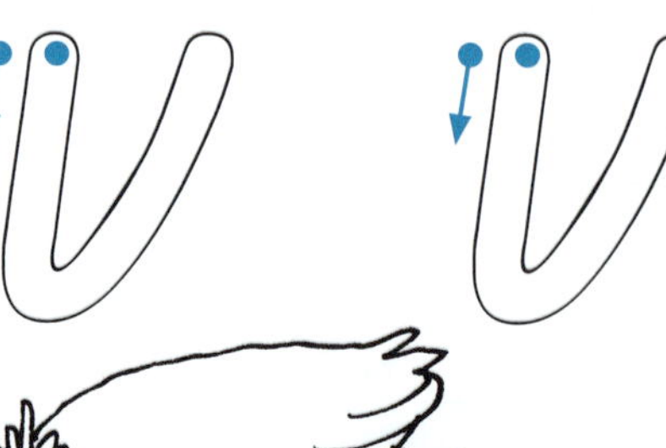

Handwriting: anticlockwise ellipse, body (short) letter v.
Vocabulary: violin, vulture, vicious.
Phonic knowledge /v/: vet, van, visit, very.

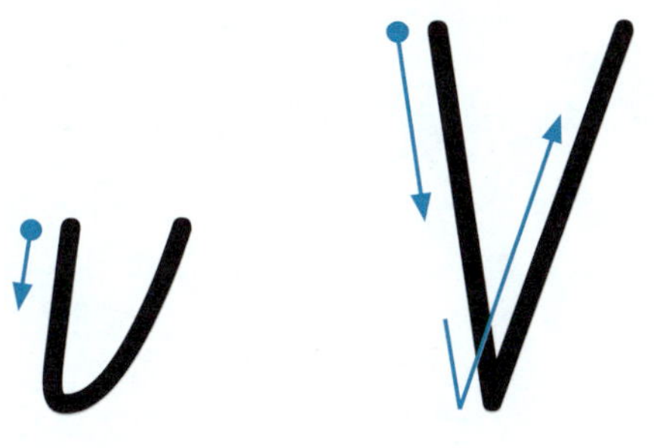

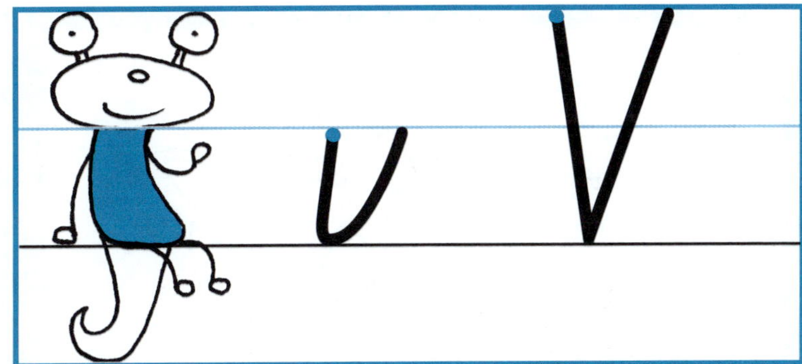

Track.

Trace.

Trace.

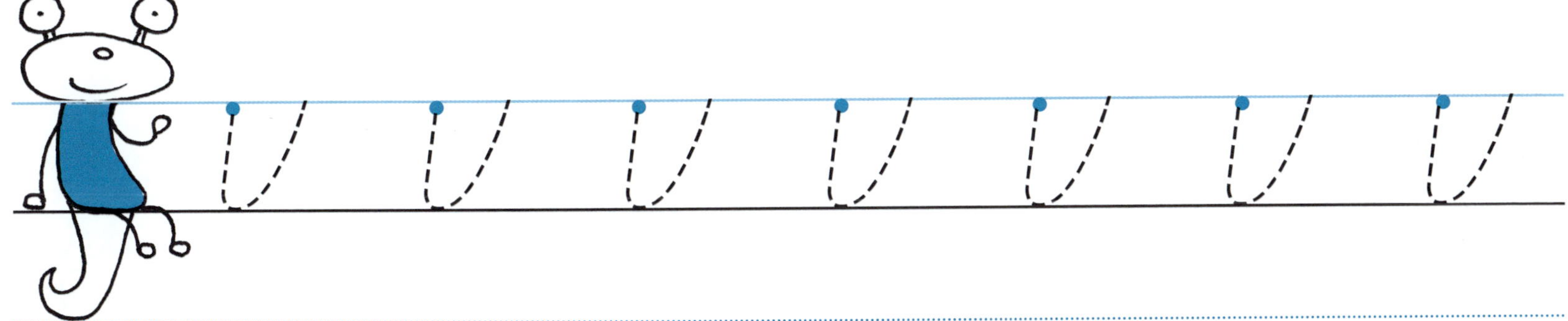

Write.

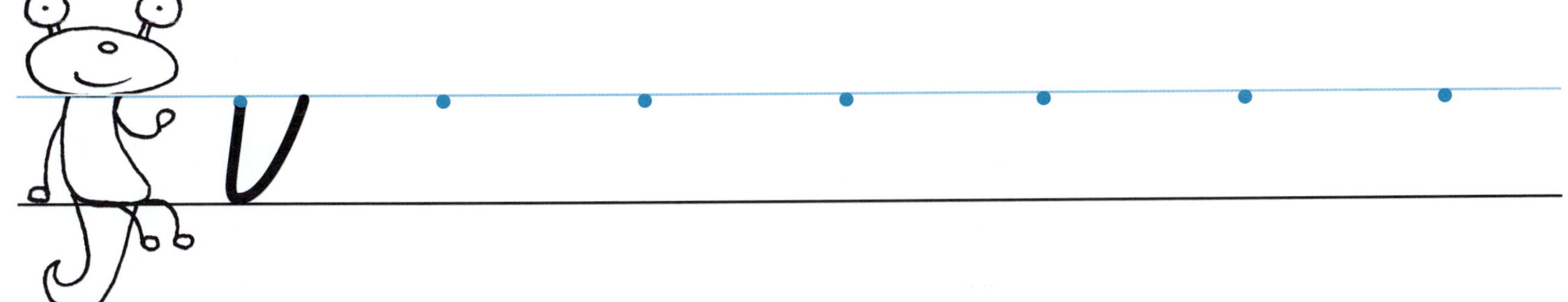

Patter

Go down, around and up. Keep your pencil on the page.

Phonic knowledge chant

wiggly wolf

w w w

Trace the pattern.

Trace the pattern. Keep your pencil on the page.

Trace the pattern. Turn each pattern into a picture.

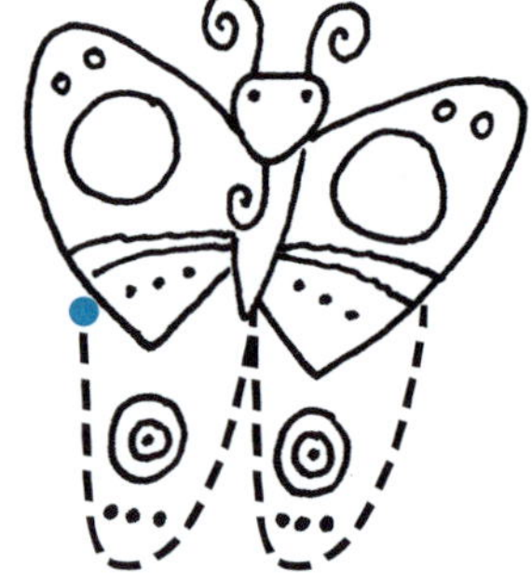

Track.

Handwriting: anticlockwise ellipse, body (short) letter w.
Vocabulary: wiggly, wings, wolf, whale, wish, when, where, why.
Phonic knowledge /w/: wet, win, we, web, went, want, was.

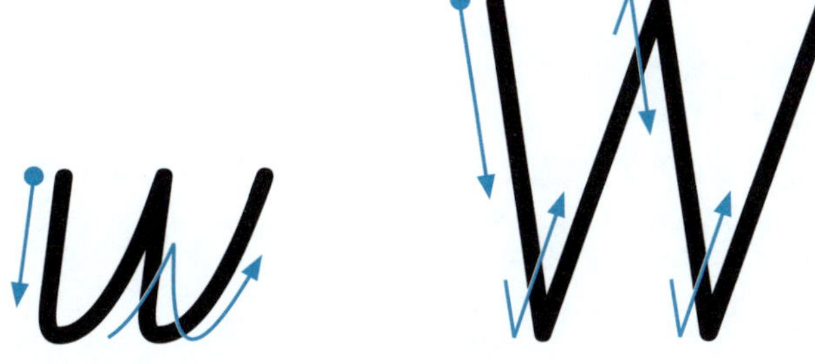
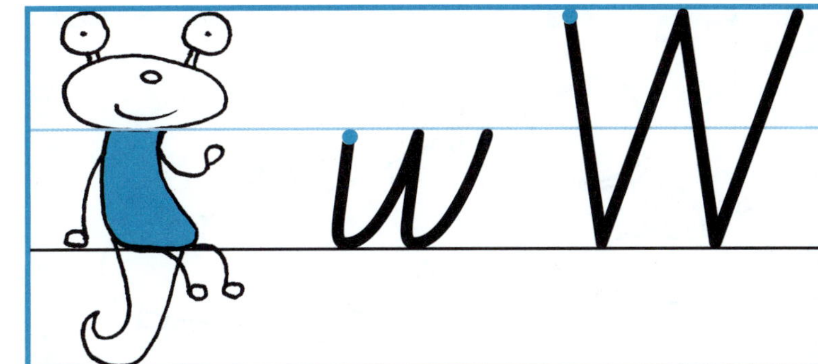

Track.

Trace.

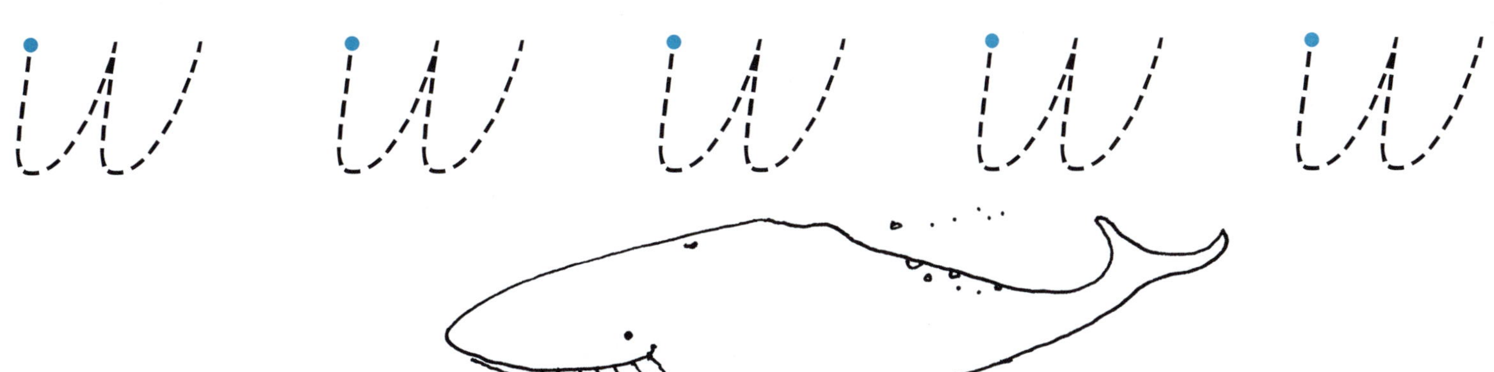

Trace.

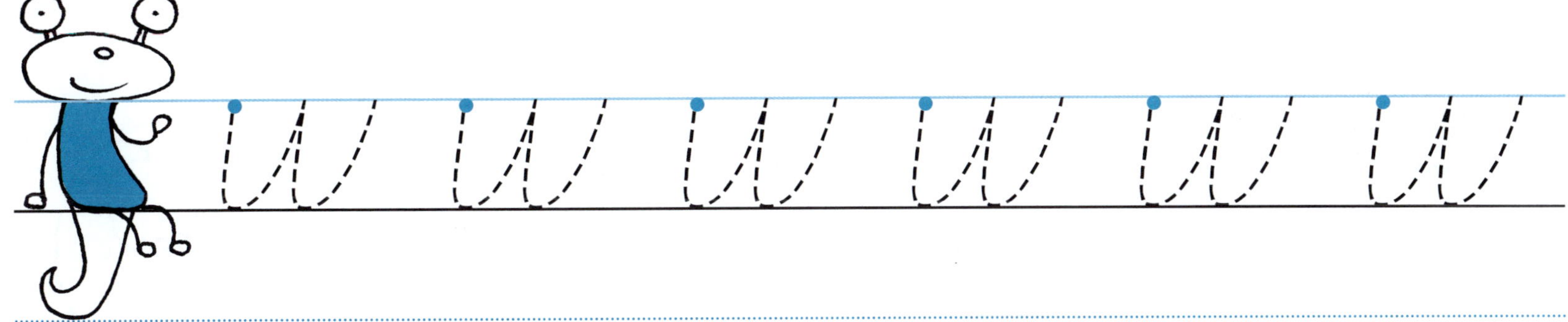

Write.

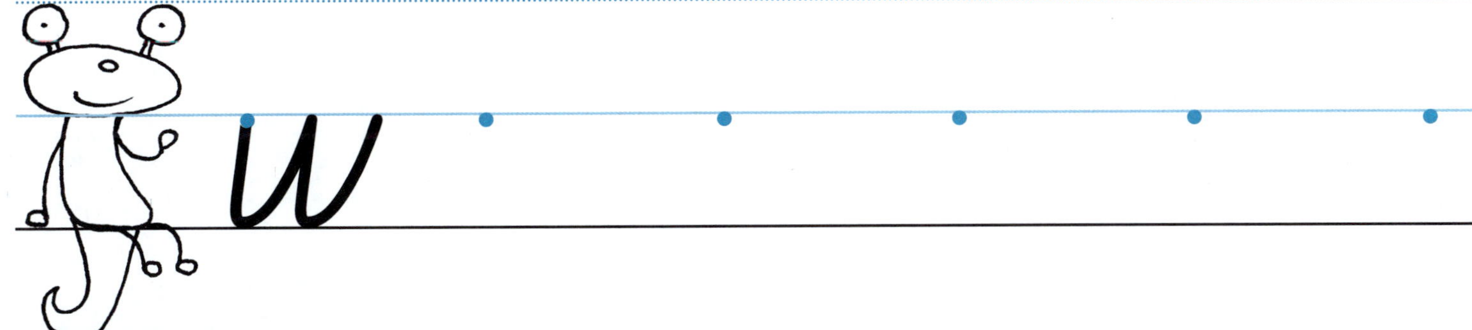

Patter Go down, around, up then down again, around and up. Keep your pencil on the page.

Phonic knowledge chant

angry alligator

a a a

Track the pattern. Keep your pencil on the page.

Trace the pattern. Keep your pencil on the page.

Trace the pattern.

Track.

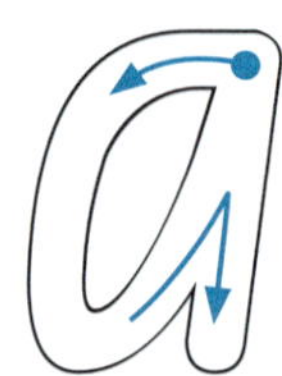

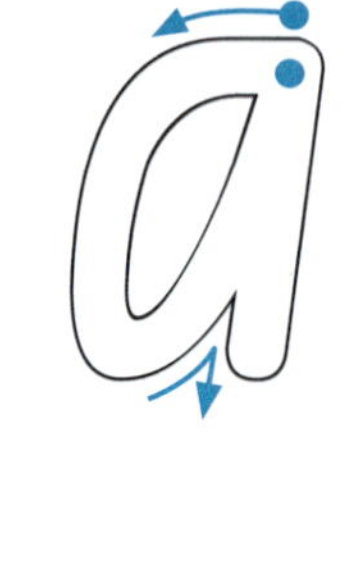

Handwriting: anticlockwise ellipse, body (short) letter a.
Vocabulary: anteater, angry, alligator, apple.
Phonic knowledge /a/: an, ant, cat, mat, sat, tap, pat.

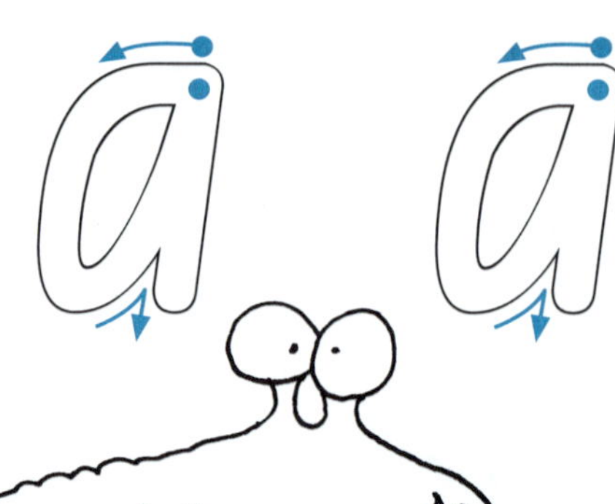

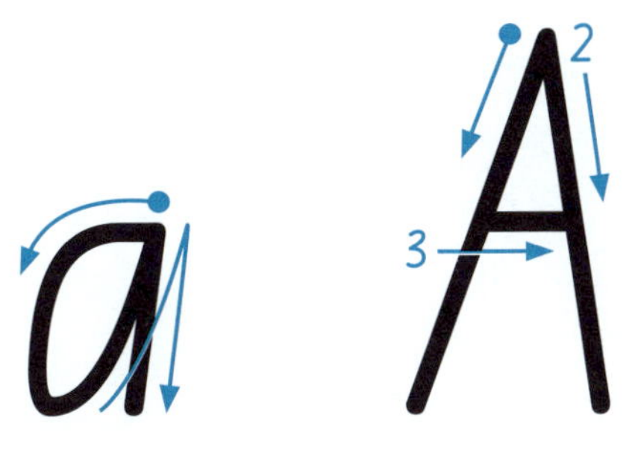

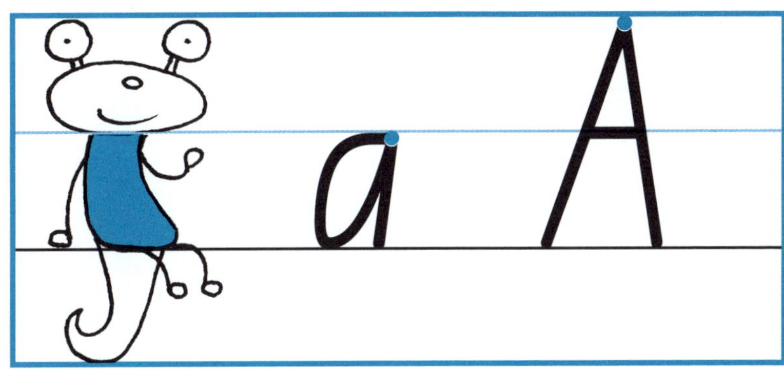

Track.

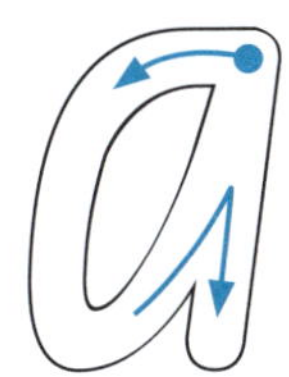      

Trace.

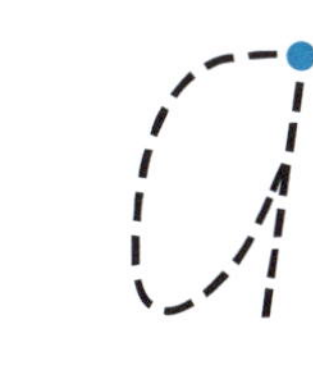   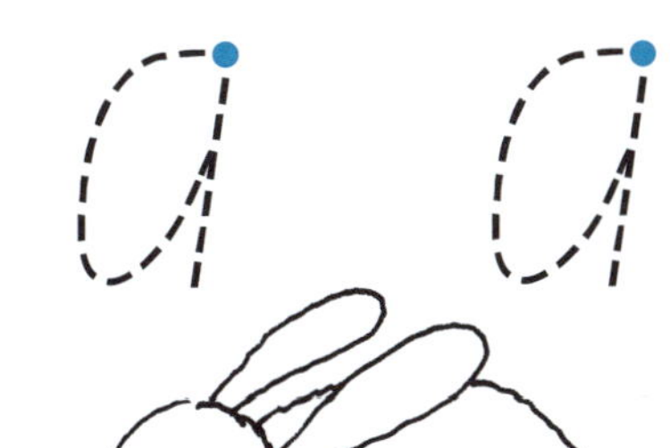 

Trace.

Write.

Patter

Go backwards then curve down, around the bottom and back up to the start, then straight down. Keep your pencil on the page.

Phonic knowledge chant

giggly goanna

g g g

Trace the pattern.

Trace the pattern.

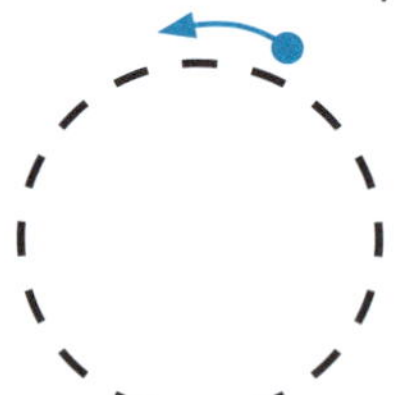 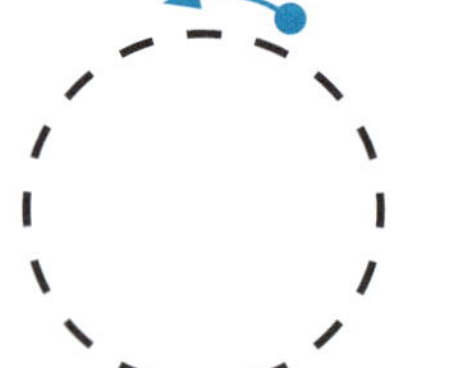  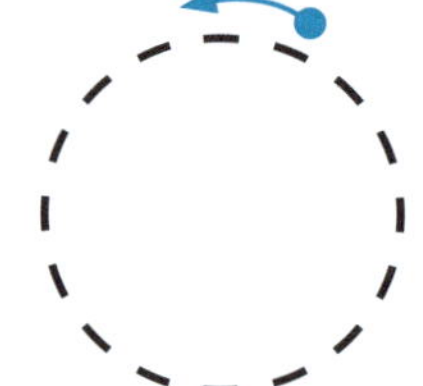 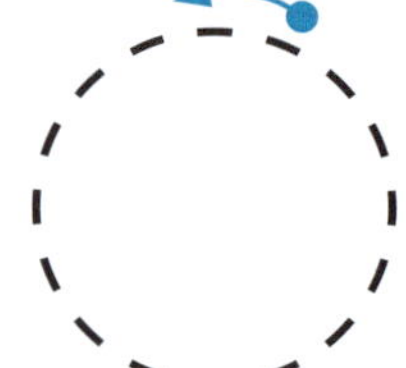 

Trace the pattern.

Track.

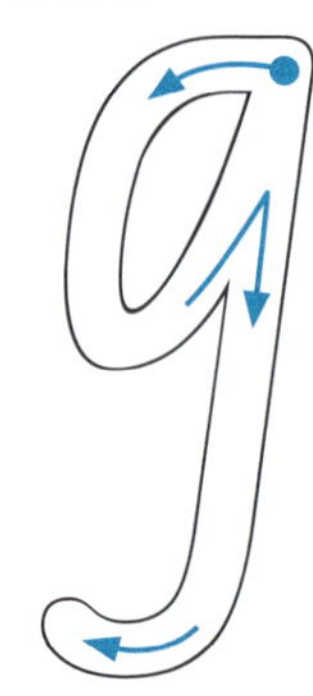 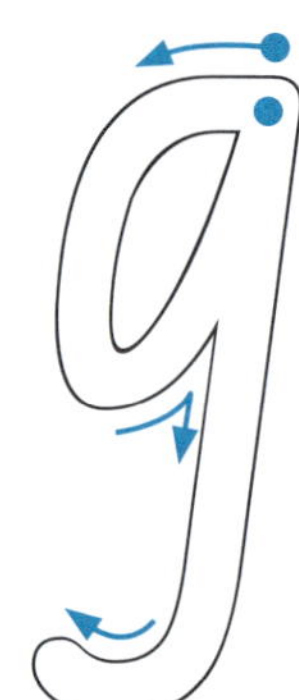 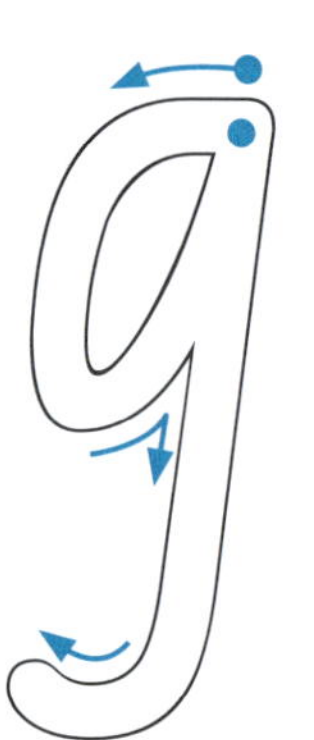 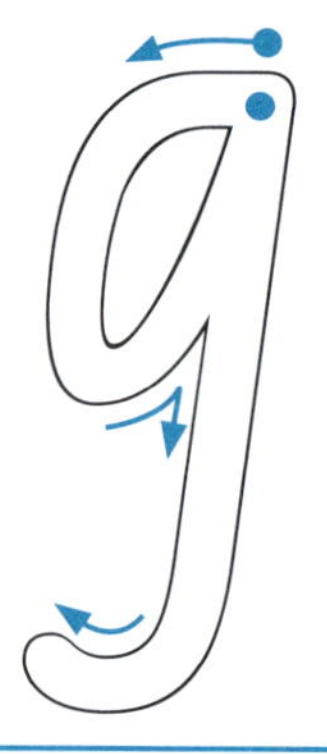 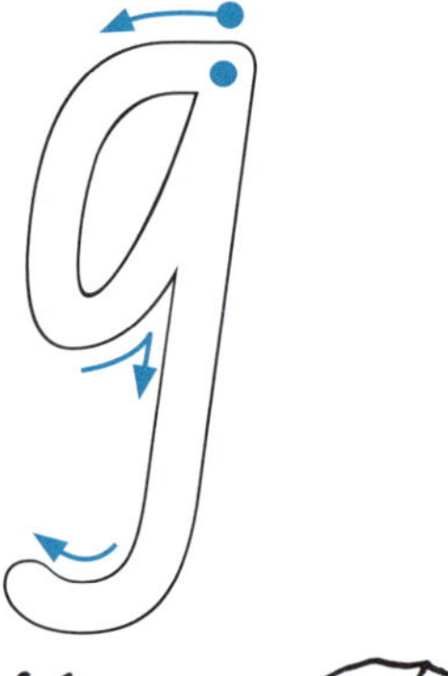 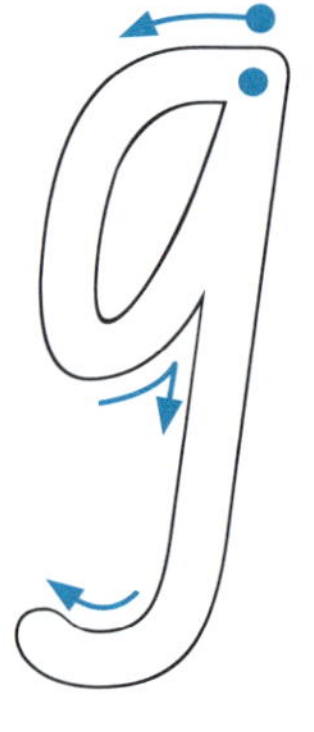

Handwriting: anticlockwise ellipse, body and tail (long) letter g.
Vocabulary: giggly, goanna.
Phonic knowledge /g/: get, go, got, gas, pig, dig, dog, hog, tag, sag, egg.

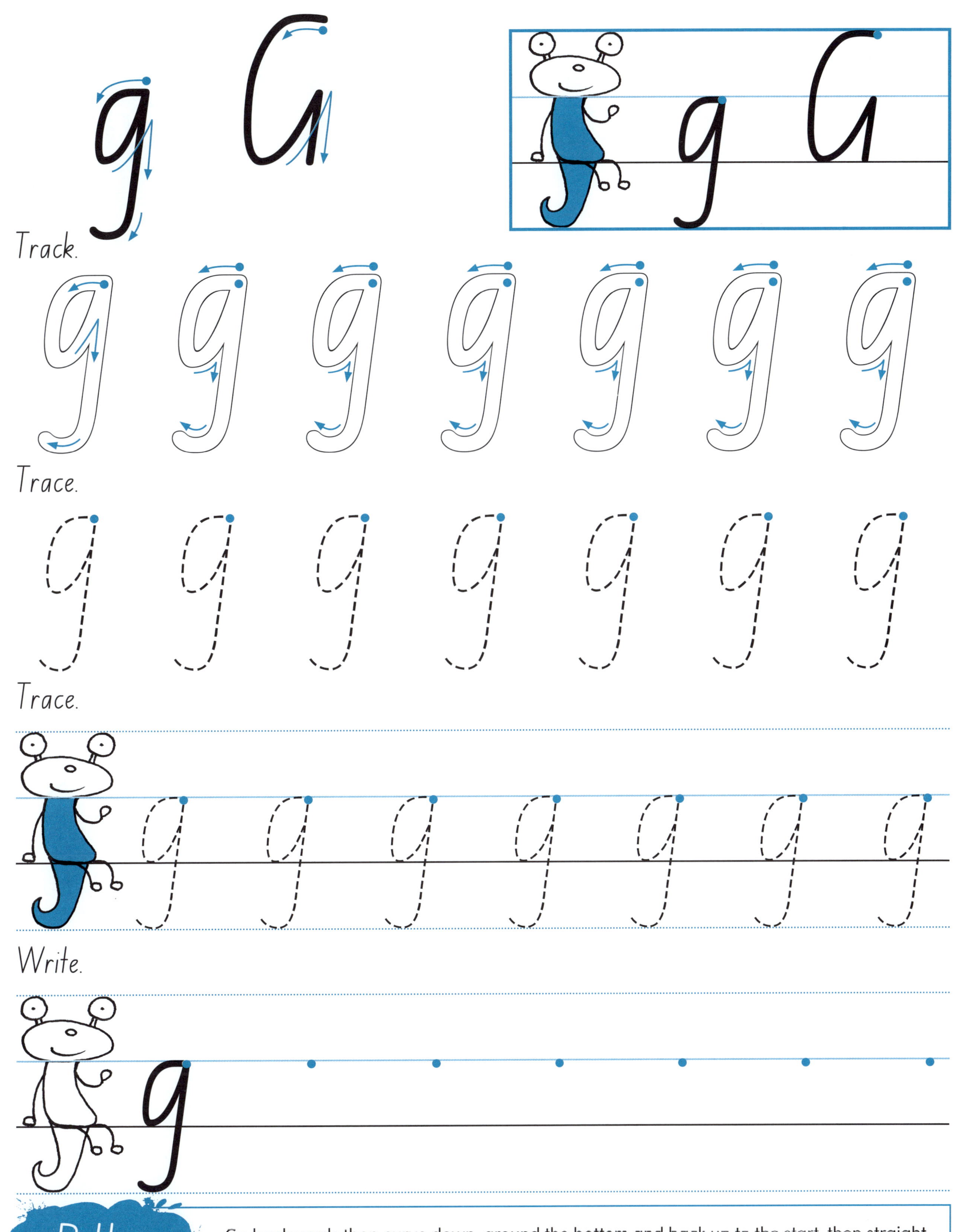

Patter

Go backwards then curve down, around the bottom and back up to the start, then straight down to make a tail. Keep your pencil on the page.

Phonic knowledge chant

quick quokkas
qu qu qu

Trace the pattern. Keep your pencil on the page.

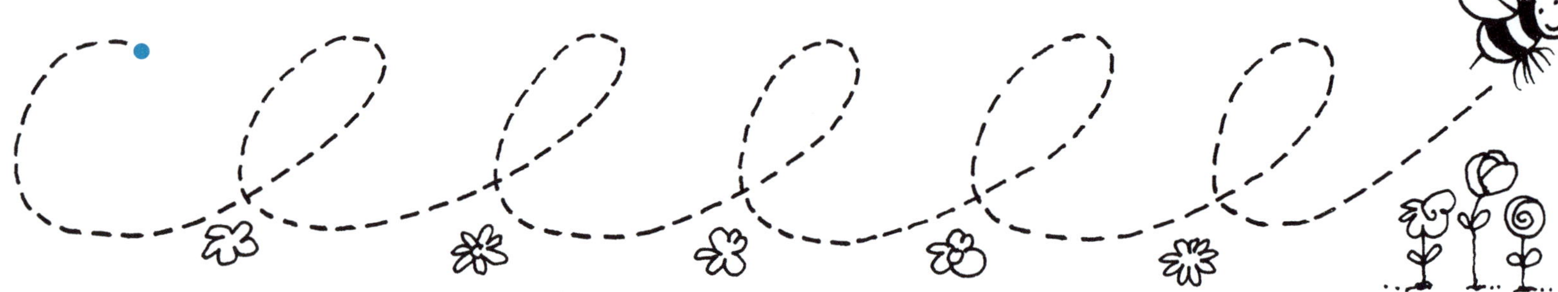

Trace the pattern. Keep your pencil on the page.

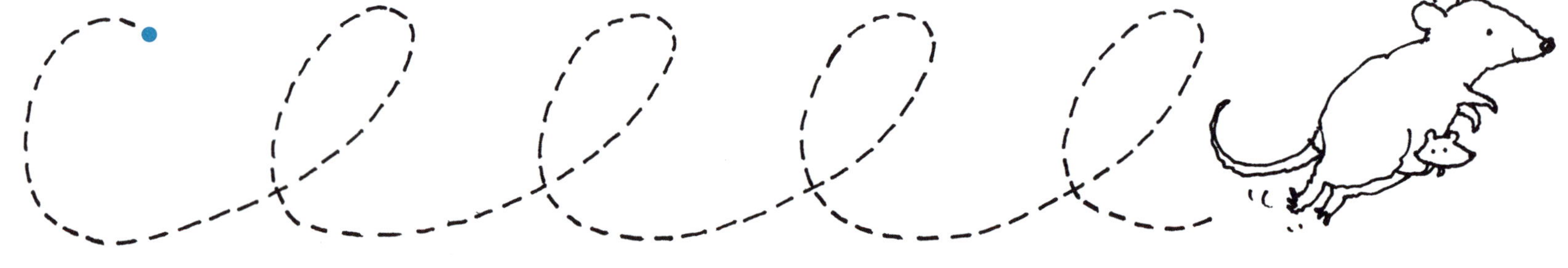

Trace.

Track.

Handwriting: anticlockwise ellipse, body and tail (long) letter q.
Vocabulary: quick, quokka. The word "quokka" is based on the word "gwagga" from the Noongar language.
Phonic knowledge /kw/: quick, quack, quiz.

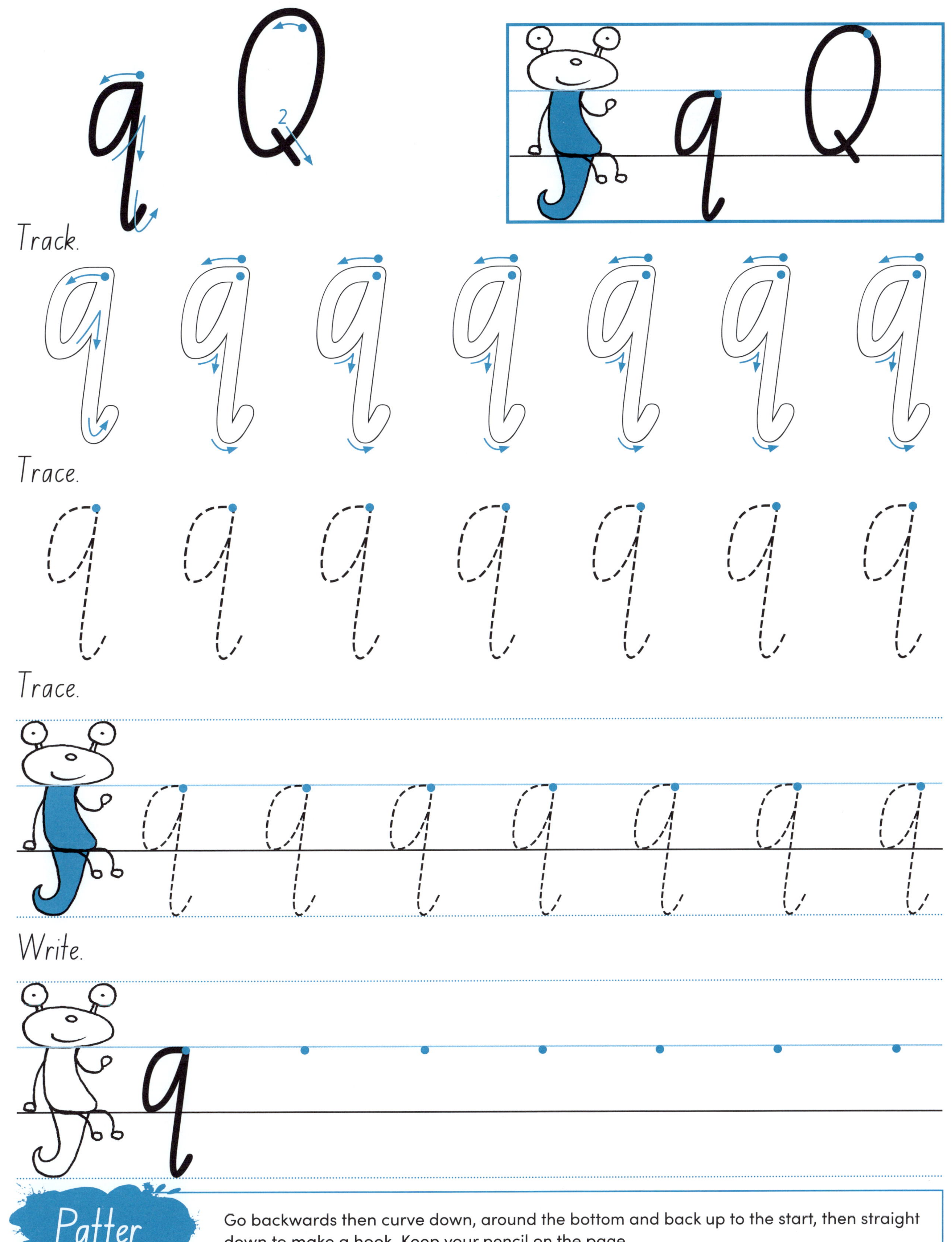

Patter

Go backwards then curve down, around the bottom and back up to the start, then straight down to make a hook. Keep your pencil on the page.

Phonic knowledge chant

cool cow

c c c

Trace the pattern.

Find c.

Track.

 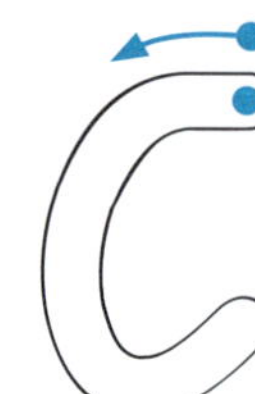 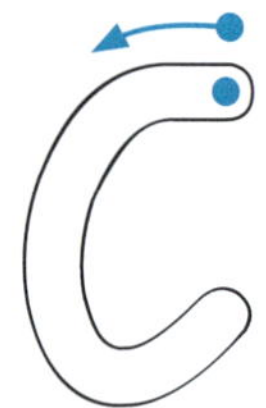 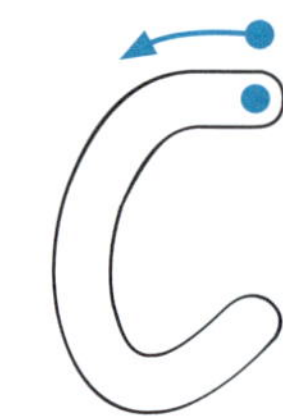  

Handwriting: anticlockwise ellipse, body (short) letter c.
Vocabulary: cool, cow, cake, candle.
Phonic knowledge /k/: cat, can, cap, cup, cot, come.

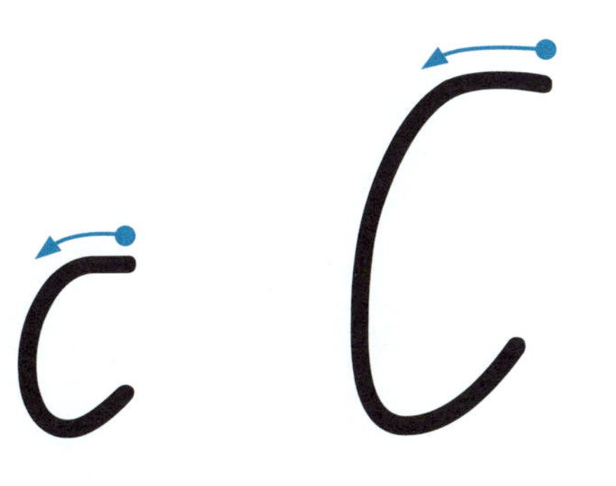
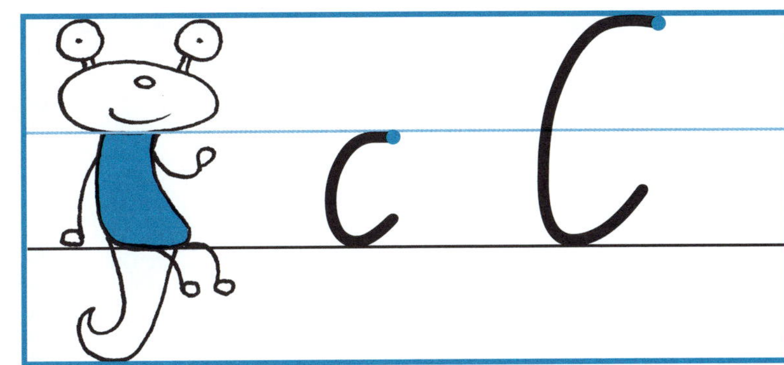

Track.

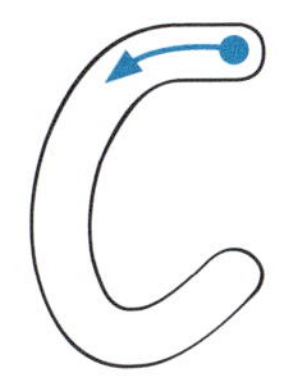  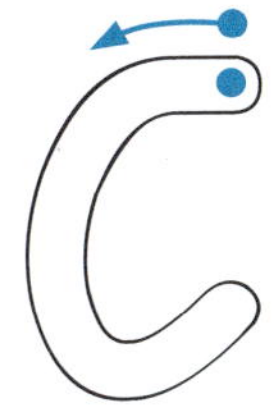    

Trace.

 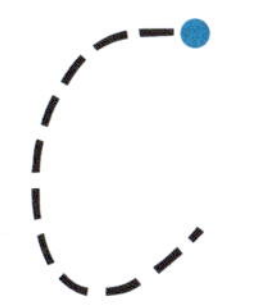  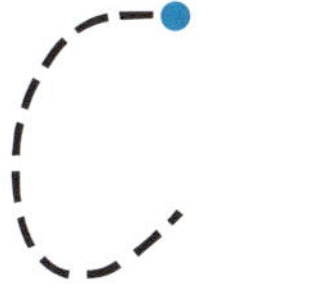   

Trace.

 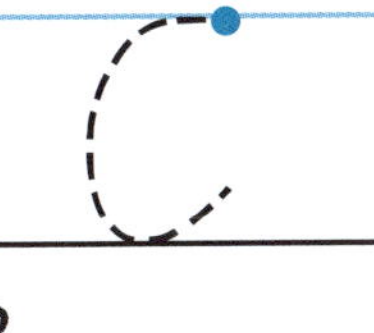 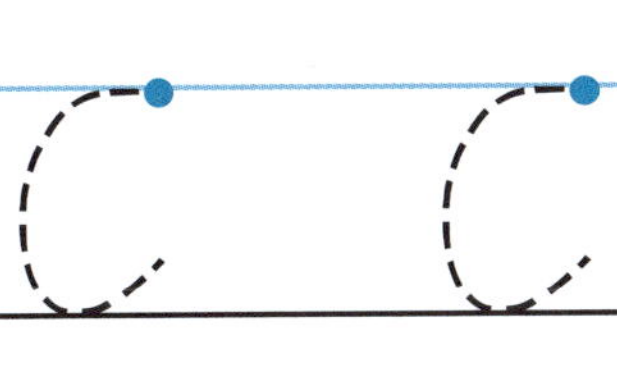  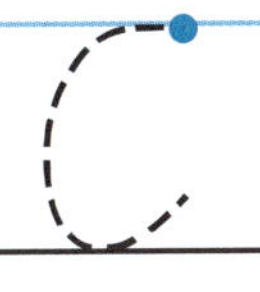 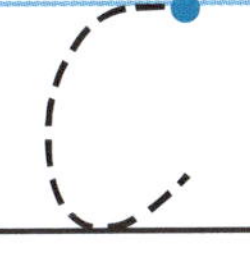 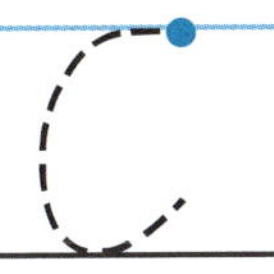 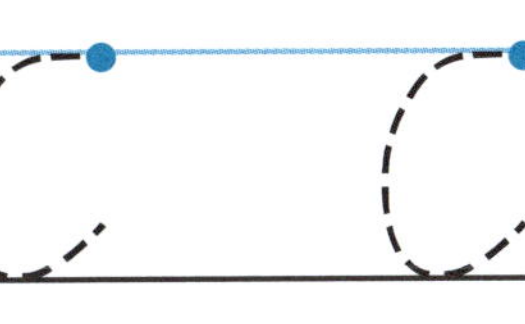

Write.

Go backwards then curve down, around the bottom and up about halfway. Keep your pencil on the page.

Phonic knowledge chant

orange octopus

o o o

Trace the pattern.

   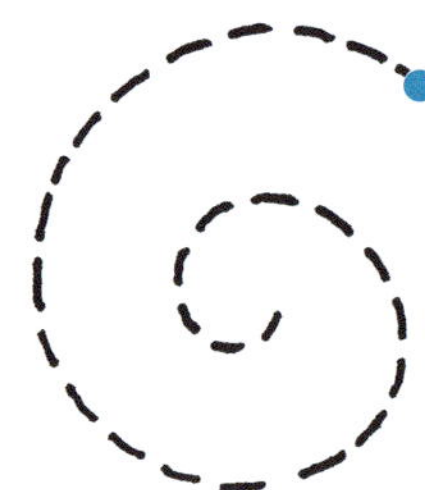 

Trace the pattern. Keep your pencil on the page.

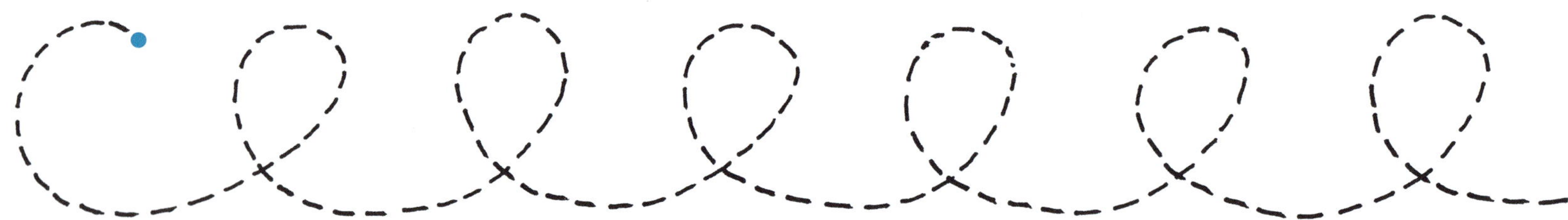

Trace the pattern.

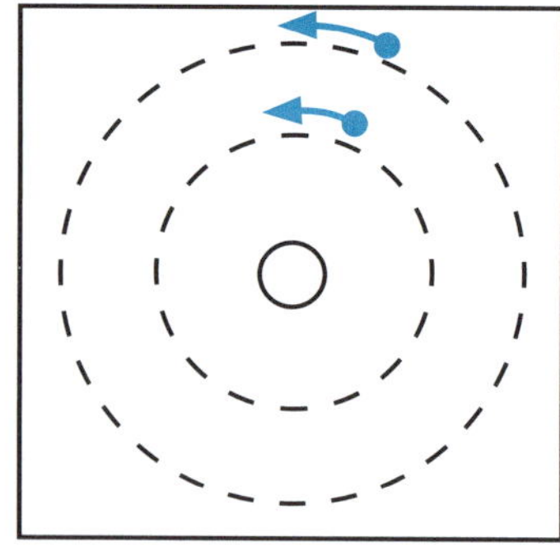 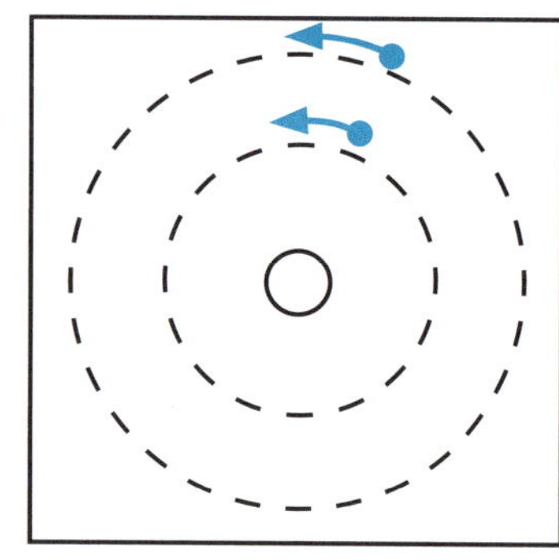 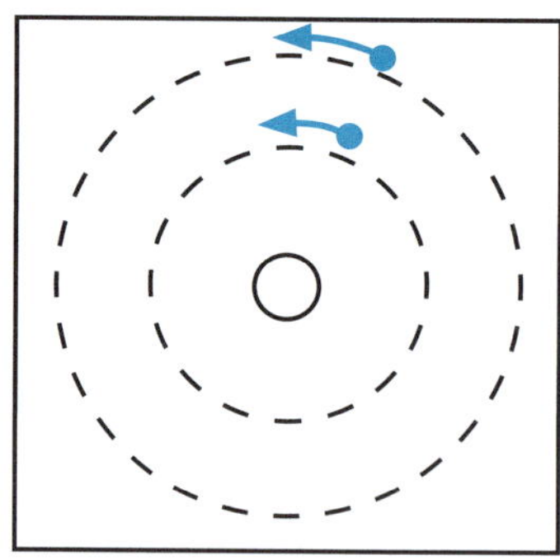 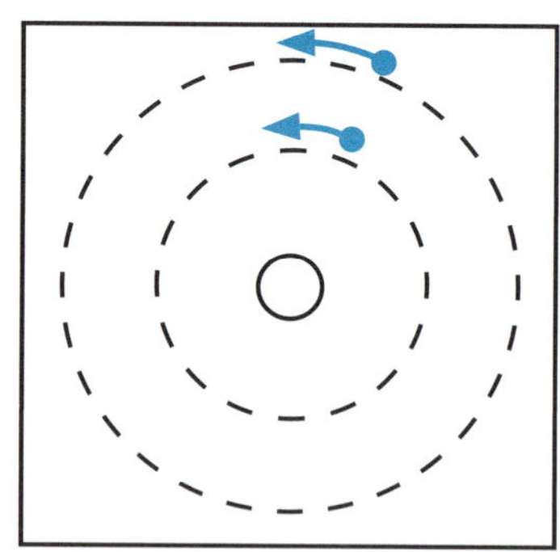

Track.

Handwriting: anticlockwise ellipse, body (short) letter o.
Vocabulary: orange, octopus.
Phonic knowledge /o/: of, on, not, got, hot, pot, log, pop, top, mop, stop.

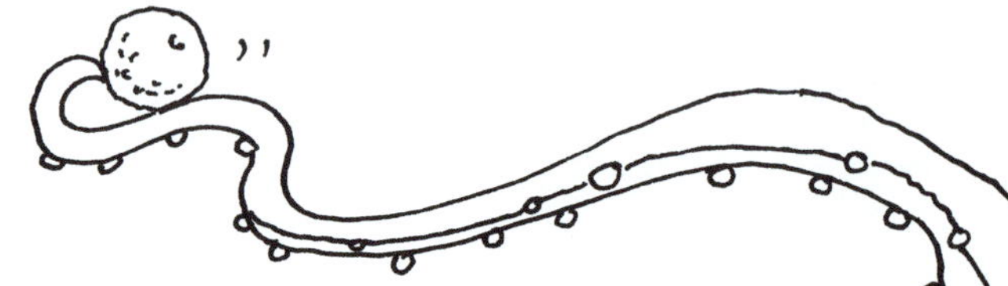

Patter

Go backwards then curve down, around the bottom and up to join where you started.
Keep your pencil on the page.

Phonic knowledge chant

slippery seal

s s s

Trace the pattern.

Trace the pattern. Turn the pattern into snakes.

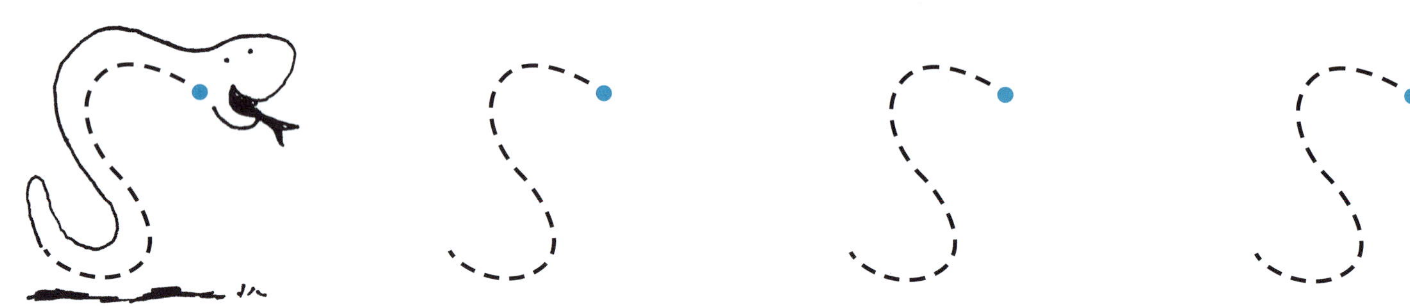

Trace the pattern. Keep your pencil on the page.

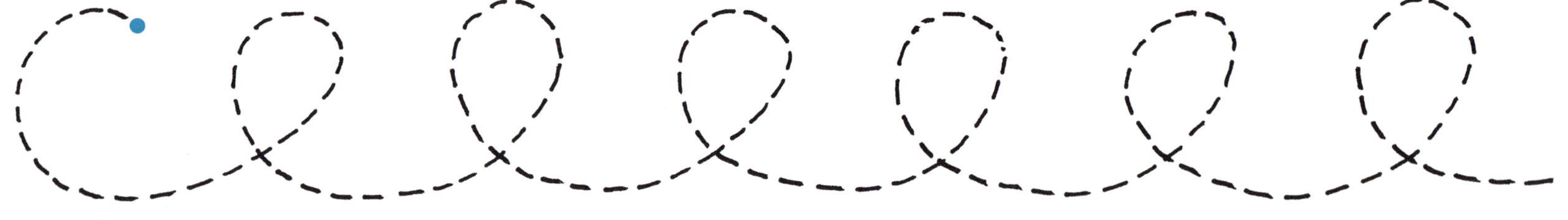

Track.

Handwriting: anticlockwise ellipse, body (short) letter s.
Vocabulary: snake, snail, seal, slippery, scissors, slip.
Phonic knowledge /s/: sat, sit, sip, so, six, sun.

Patter

First go backwards, then curve around and across the middle, then go around the bottom and up in a curve. Keep your pencil on the page.

Phonic knowledge chant

dirty dingo
d d d

Trace the pattern.

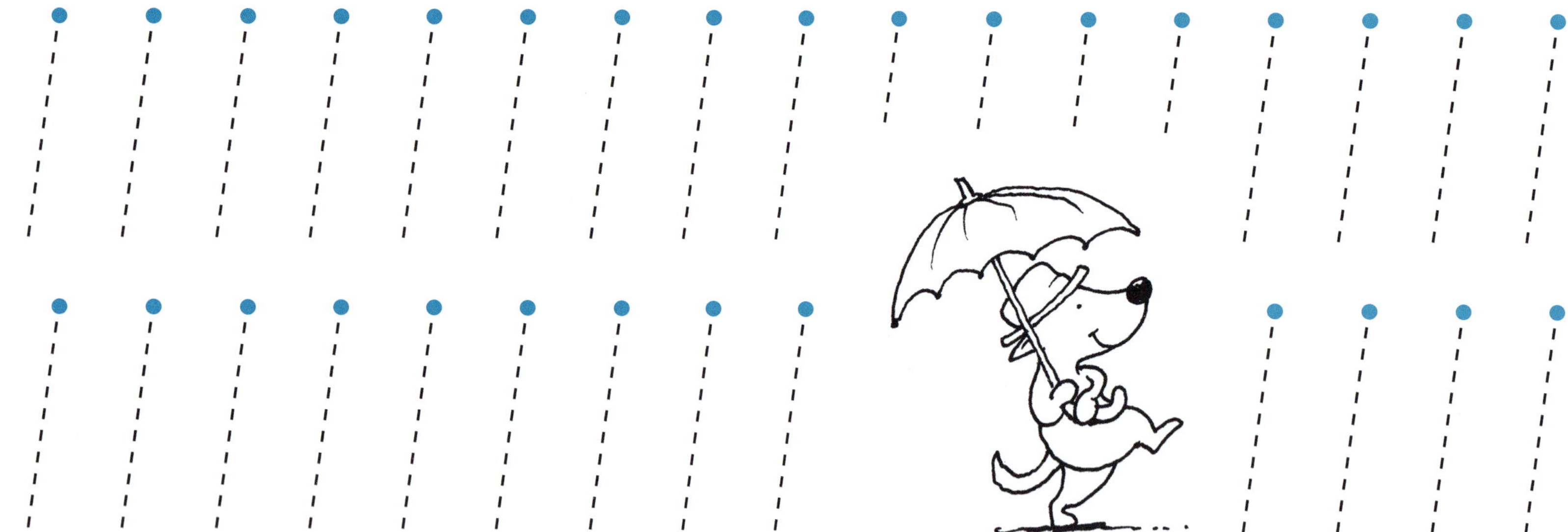

Trace the pattern.

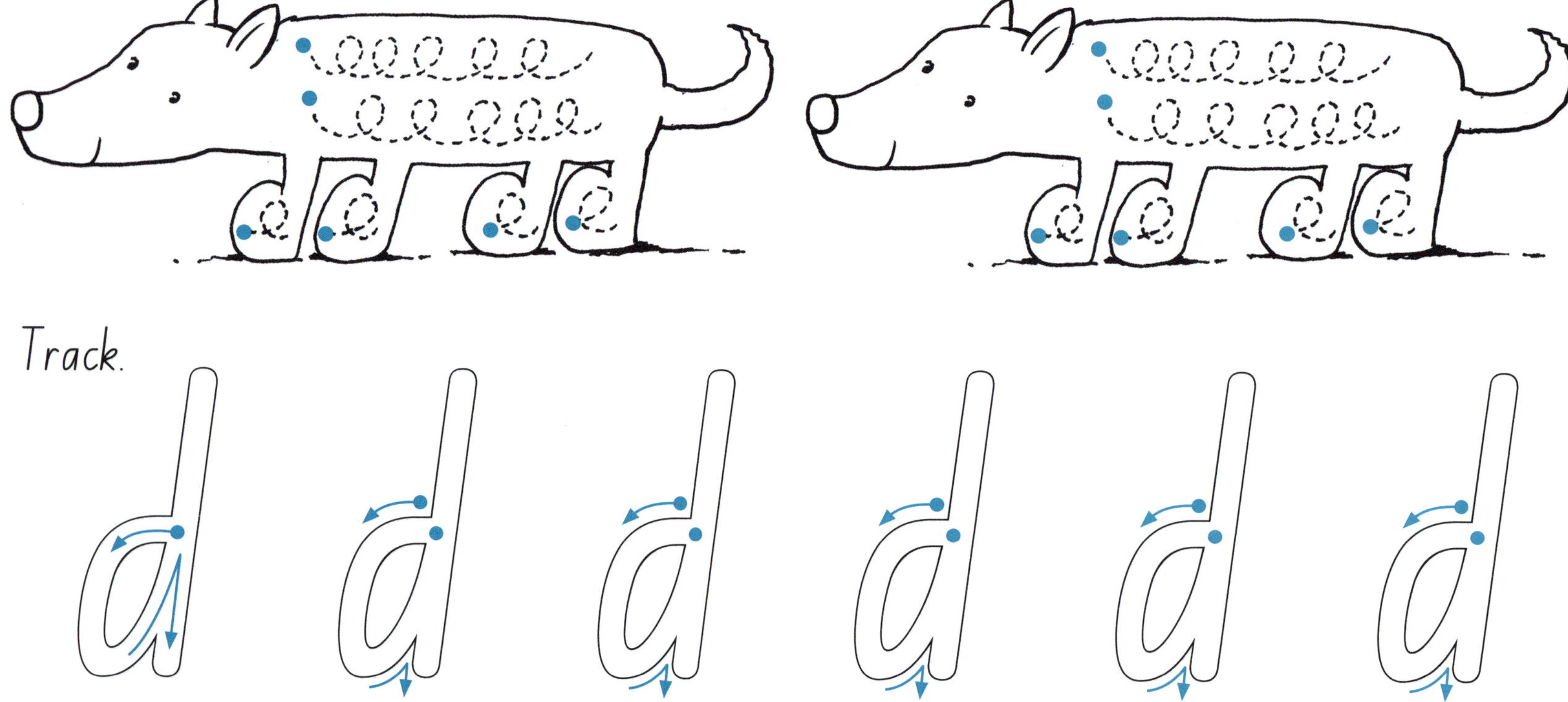

Track.

d d d d d d

Handwriting: anticlockwise ellipse, head and body (tall) letter d. **Vocabulary:** dingo, dirty, down. The word "dingo" is based on the word "dingu" from the Dharug and Dharawal languages. It means "wild dog".
Phonic knowledge /d/: do, don't, dog, din, dip, dad, did, lid, and, mad, sad, sand, stand, said.

Patter

Go backwards then curve down, around the bottom and up all the way to the top, then straight down. Keep your pencil on the page.

Phonic knowledge chant

energetic elephant

e e e

Trace the pattern. Keep your pencil on the page.

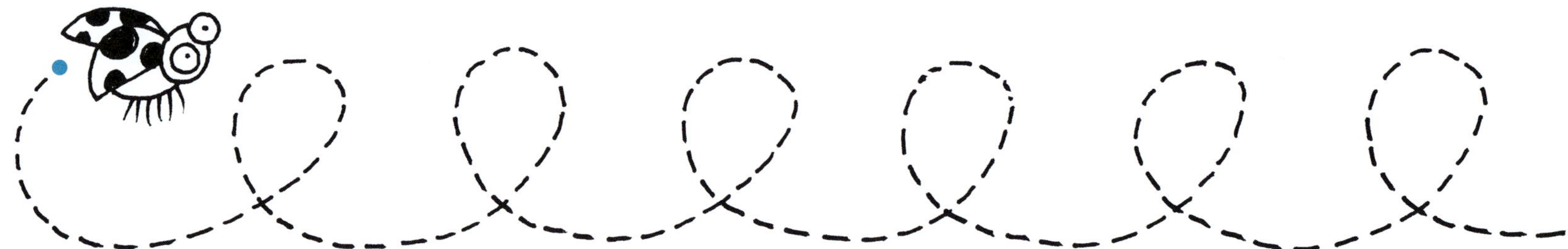

Trace the pattern.

Trace the pattern.

Track.

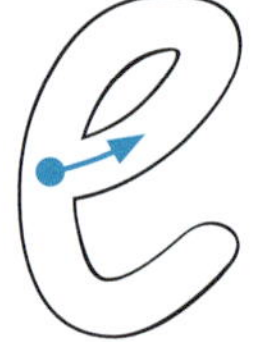

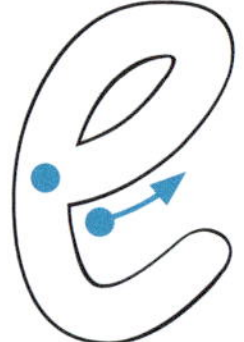
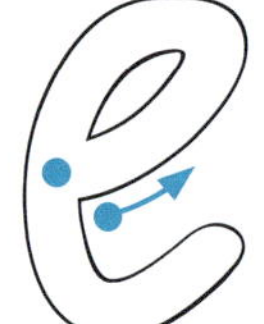

Handwriting: anticlockwise ellipse, body (short) e.
Vocabulary: elephant, energetic, eagle, eat, beetle, he, she, the.
Phonic knowledge /e/: egg, hen, men, ten, pen, met, net, get, red.

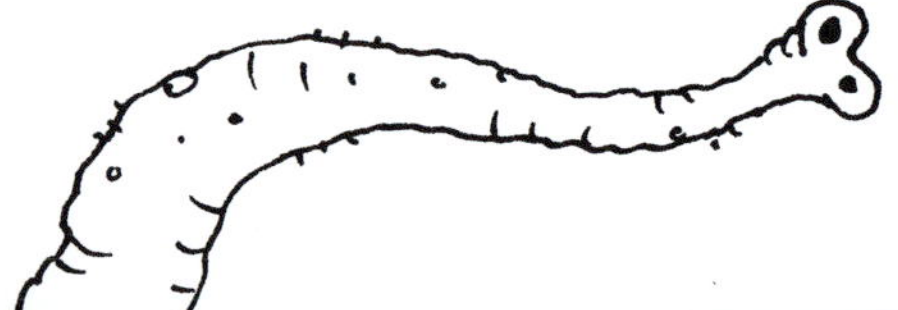

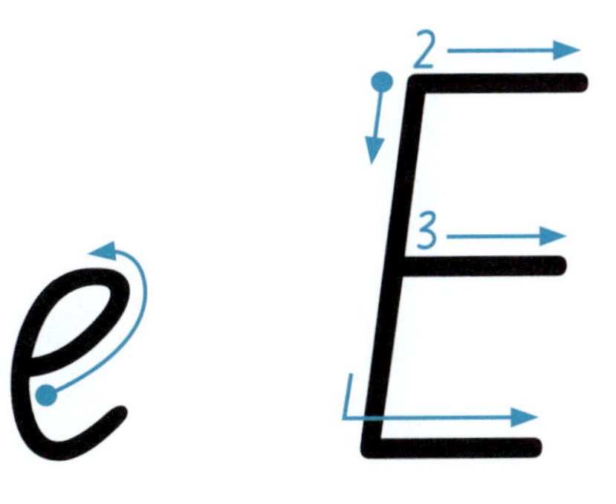
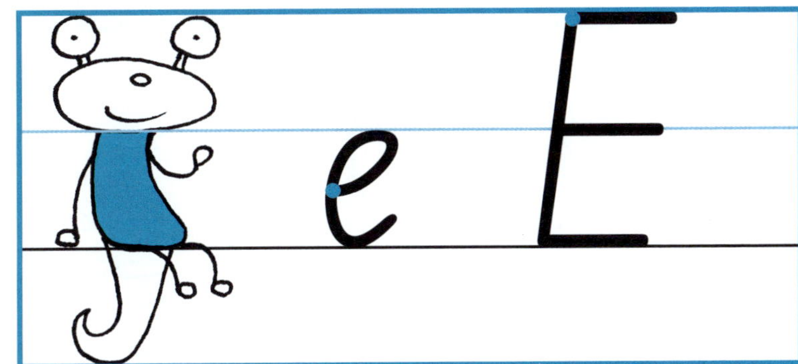

Track.

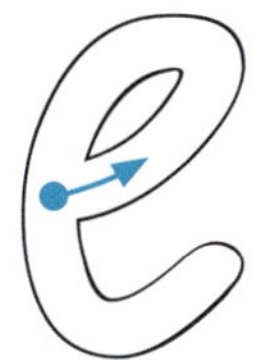      

Trace.

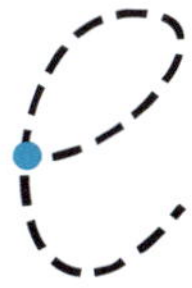  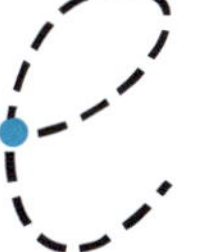 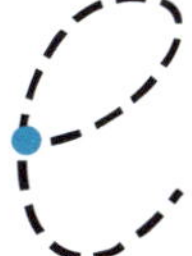   

Trace.

  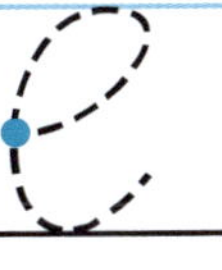 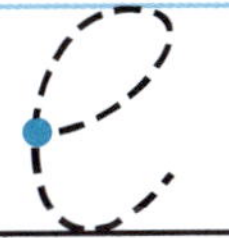 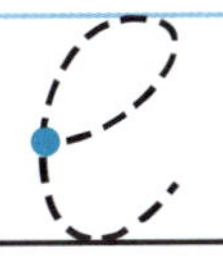 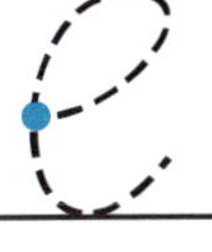  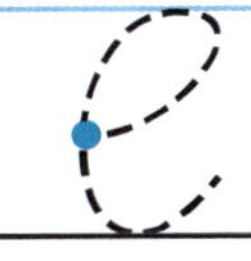

Write.

  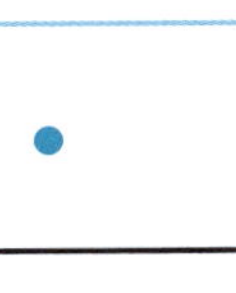     

Patter

Start in the middle, make a loop, up over the top and around, and end half way up the space.
Keep your pencil on the page.

Phonic knowledge chant

noisy numbat

n n n

Track the pattern.

Trace the pattern. Keep your pencil on the page.

Copy the pattern. Turn each pattern into a picture.

Track.

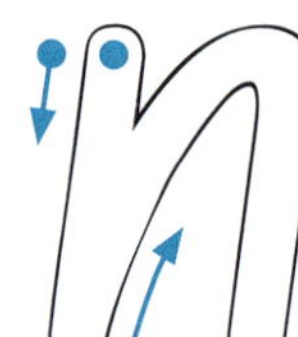

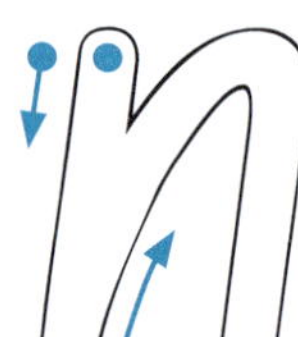

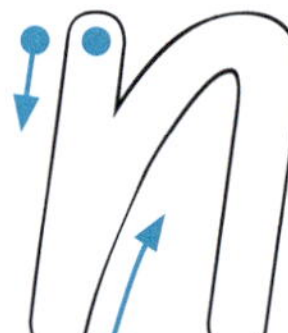

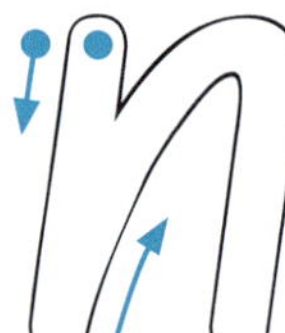

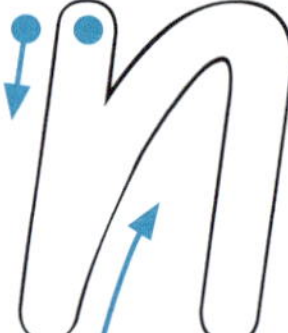

Handwriting: clockwise ellipse, body (short) letter n.
Vocabulary: noisy, numbat. The word "numbat" is based on the word "noombat" from the Noongar language.
Phonic knowledge /n/: no, not, nip, nap, nod, an, can, pan, in, pin, tin, sun, run.

Patter

Go down then up and across the top and down again. Keep your pencil on the page.

Phonic knowledge chant

rapid rat

r r r

Trace the pattern.

Find r.

Track.

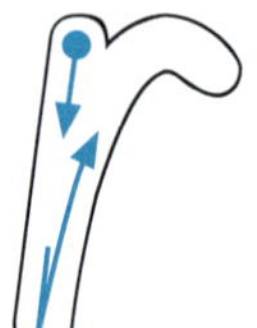 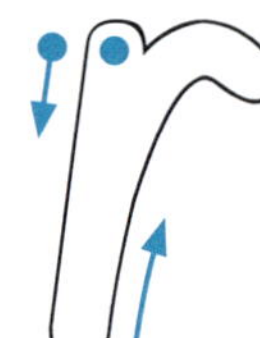 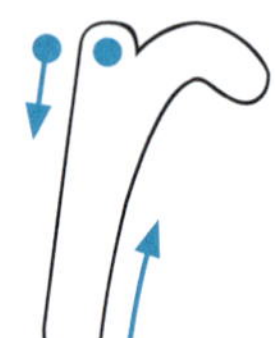 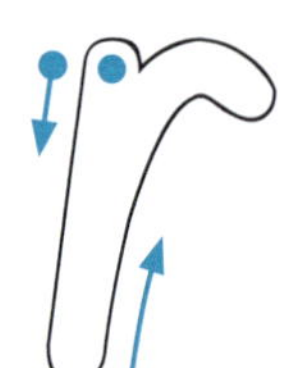 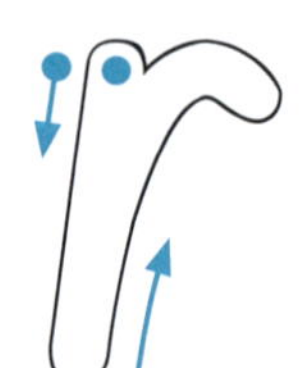 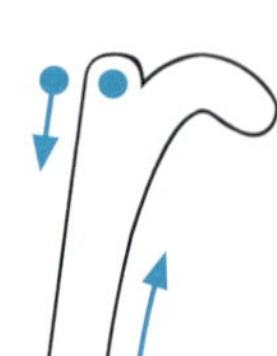

Handwriting: clockwise ellipse, body (short) letter r.
Vocabulary: race, rapid, raft.
Phonic knowledge /r/: red, rat, rip, run, ran, ram, rug, rot, drip, drop.

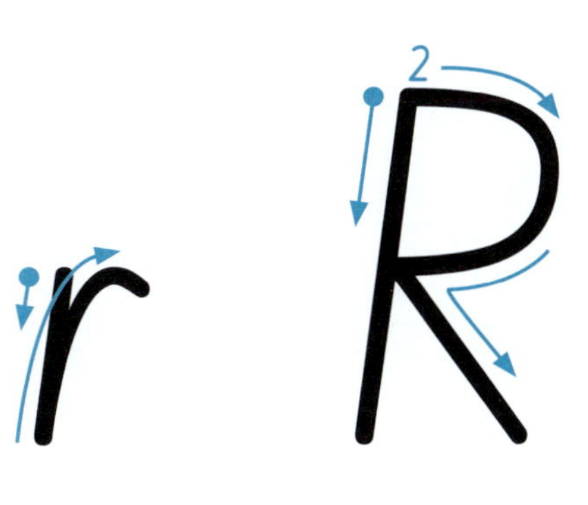

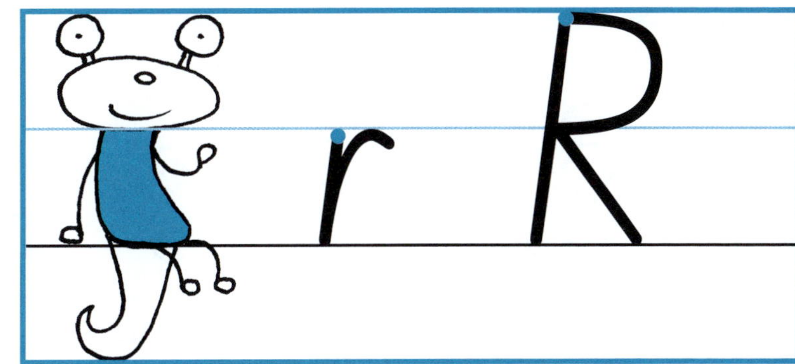

Track.

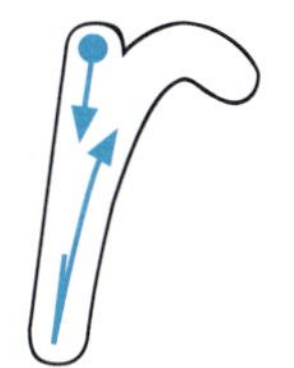 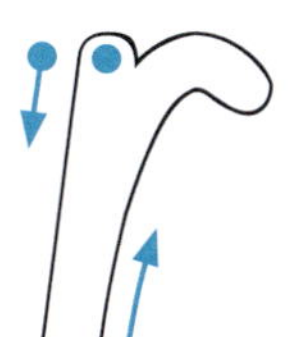 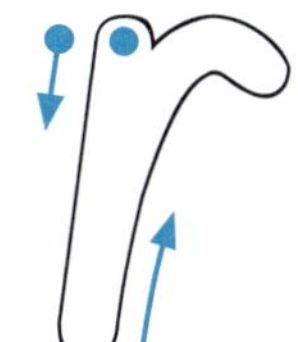 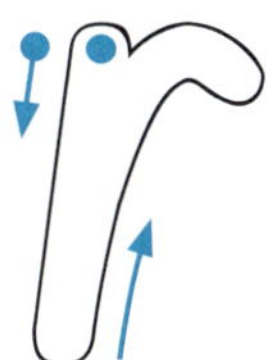 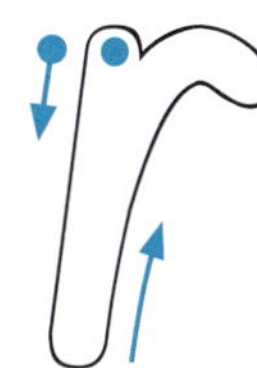 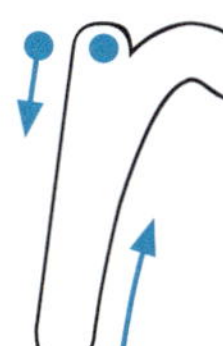 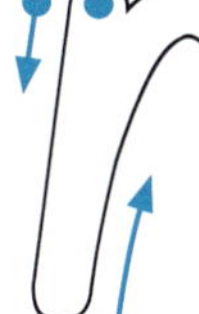

Trace.

Trace.

 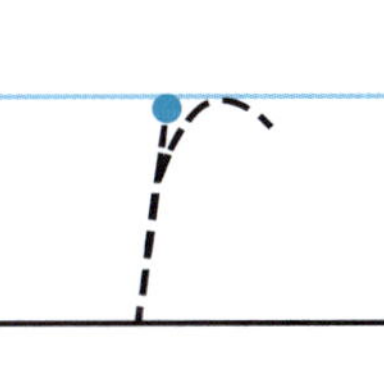 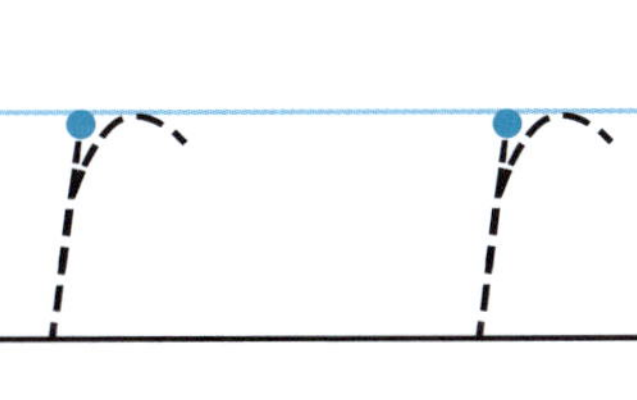 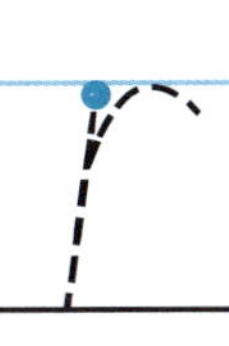 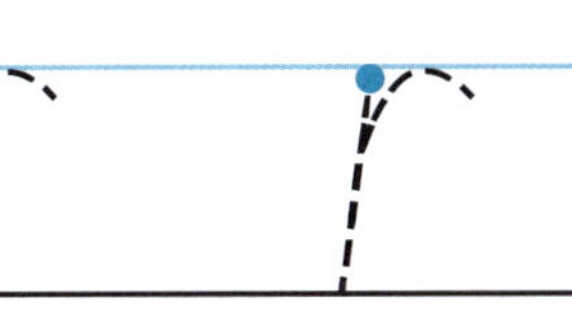 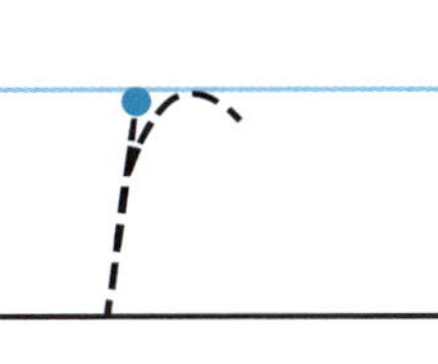

Write.

Patter

Go down then up, across the top and stop. Keep your pencil on the page.

Phonic knowledge chant

messy monkey
m m m

Trace the pattern.

Trace the pattern. Keep your pencil on the page.

m

Trace the pattern. Turn each pattern into a picture.

Track.

Handwriting: clockwise ellipse, body (short) letter m.
Vocabulary: messy, monkey, many, munch.
Phonic knowledge /m/: my, mat, map, mop, man, am, mum, men, him.

Patter

Go down then bounce up and across the top and make a second downward diagonal stroke, then bounce up and across the top and make a third downward diagonal stroke. Keep your pencil on the page.

Phonic knowledge chant

hairy hen
h h h

Trace the pattern.

Trace the pattern. Keep your pencil on the page.

Trace then copy the pattern.

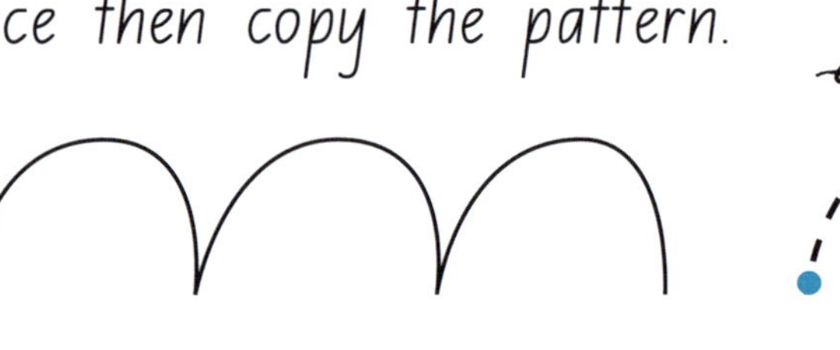
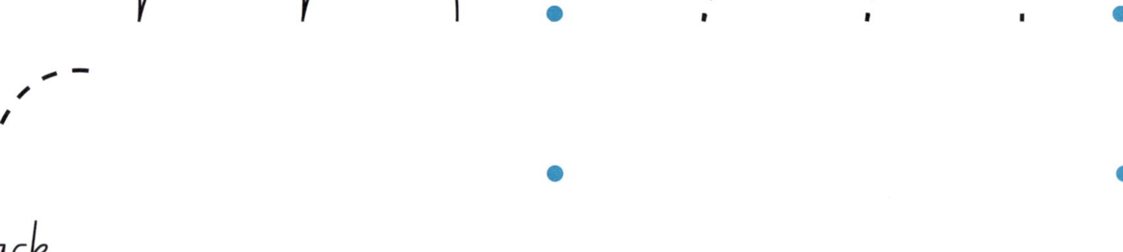

Track.

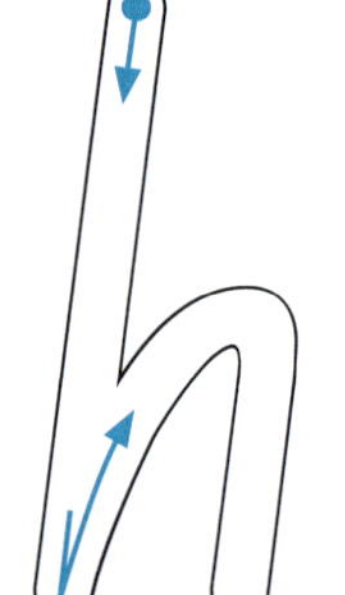    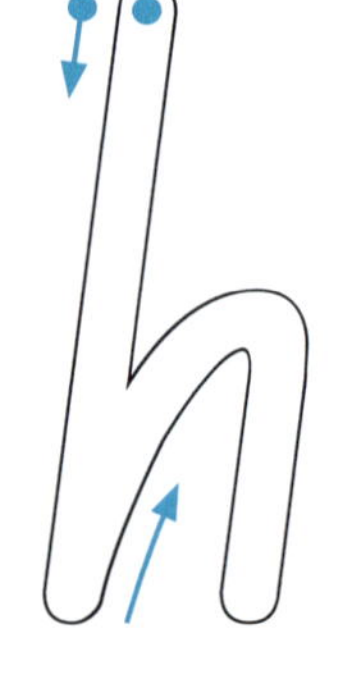 

Handwriting: clockwise ellipse, head and body (tall) letter h.
Vocabulary: hay, hairy, have, help.
Phonic knowledge /h/: hen, hop, hat, hot, hit, hug, hum, he, him, has, had.

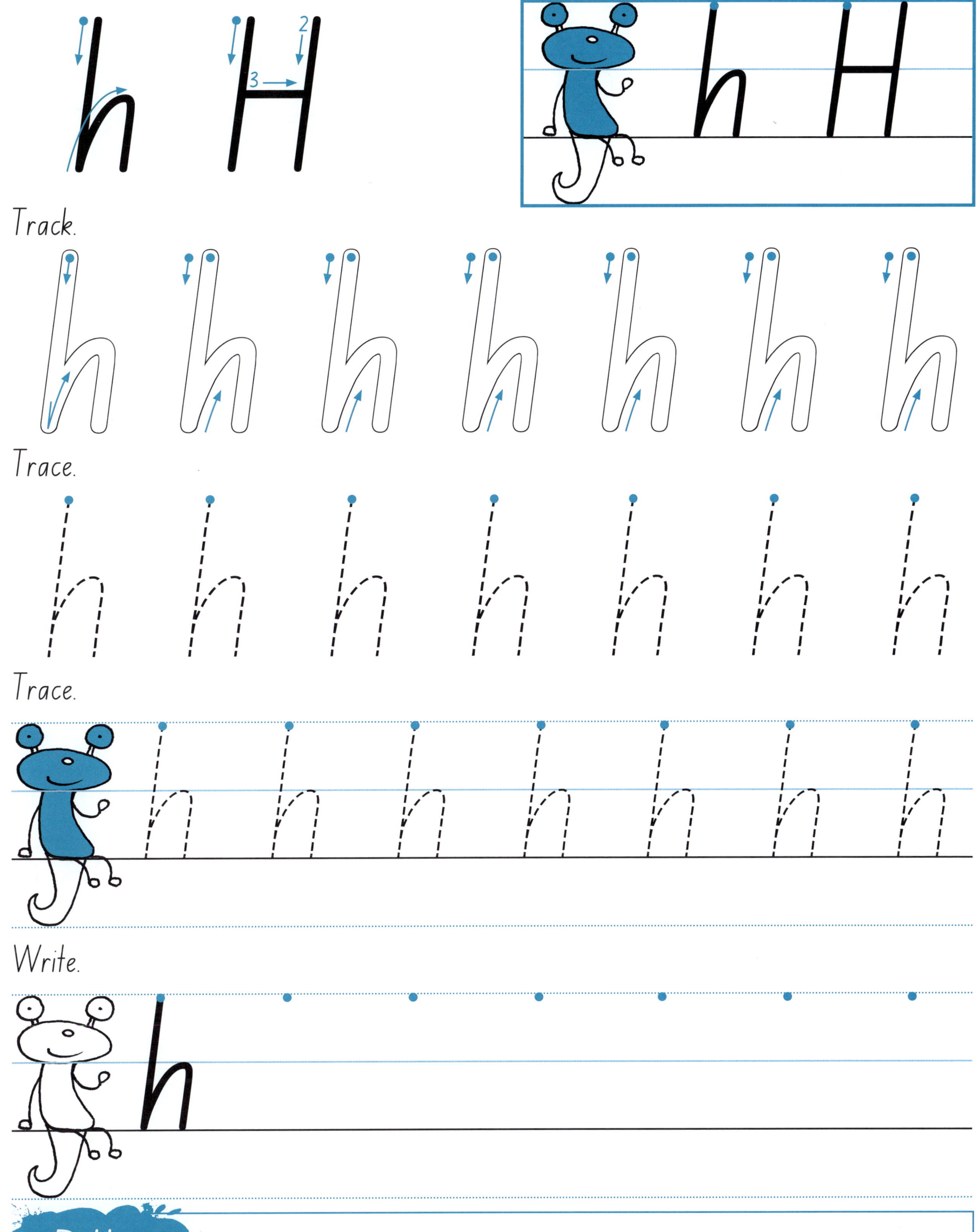

Patter

Go down then come half way up, curve around and down. Keep your pencil on the page.

Phonic knowledge chant

kind koala

k k k

Trace the pattern. Finish the kites.

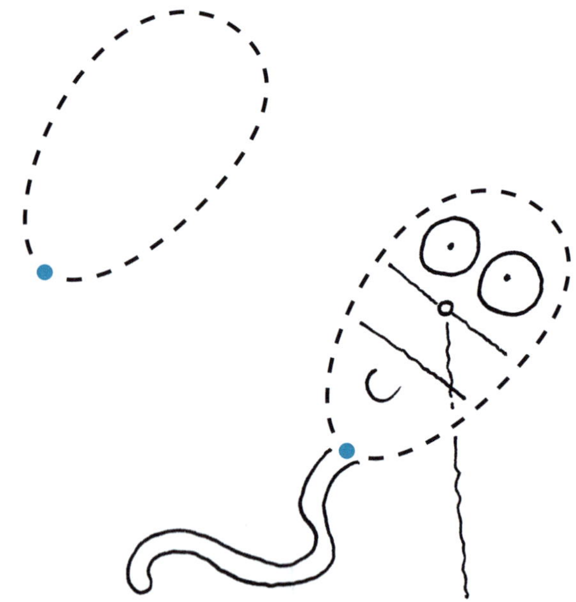

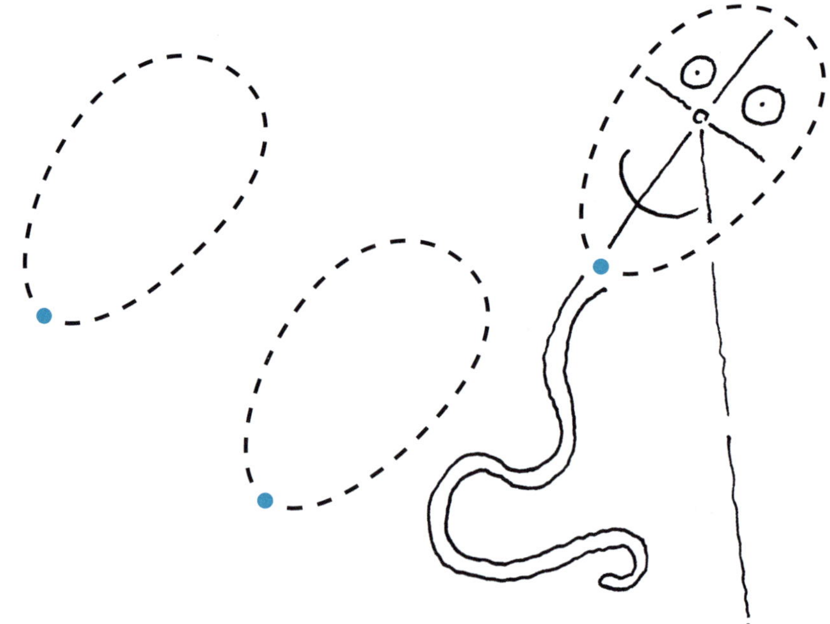

Trace the pattern. Find and write k.

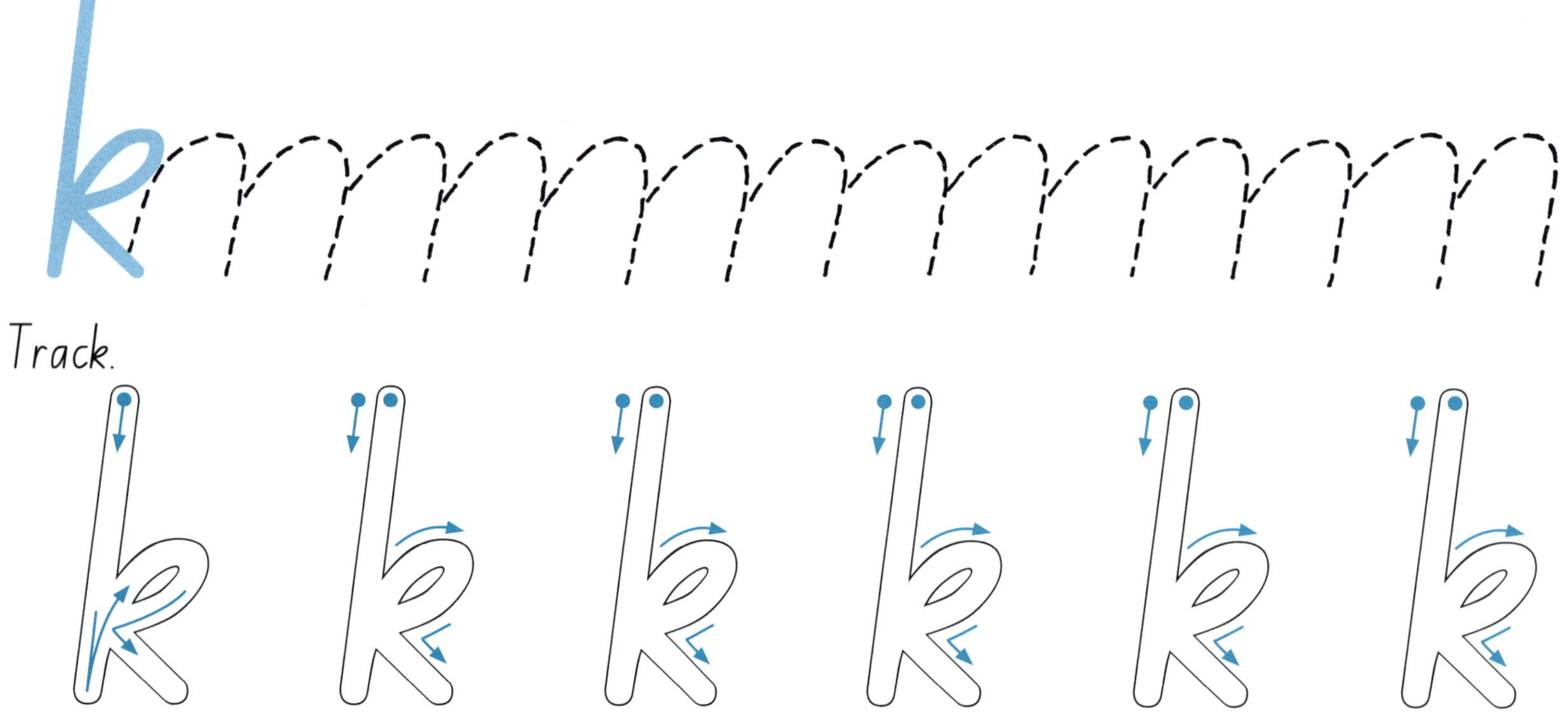

Handwriting: clockwise ellipse, head and body (tall) letter k. **Vocabulary:** kind, koala, kangaroo, kite, key, kitten. The word "koala" is based on the word "gula" from the Dharug language. Gula means "no water".
Phonic knowledge /k/: kit, king, kid.

Patter

Go down, come half way up, curve around to make a loop, then go out and end on the line. Keep your pencil on the page.

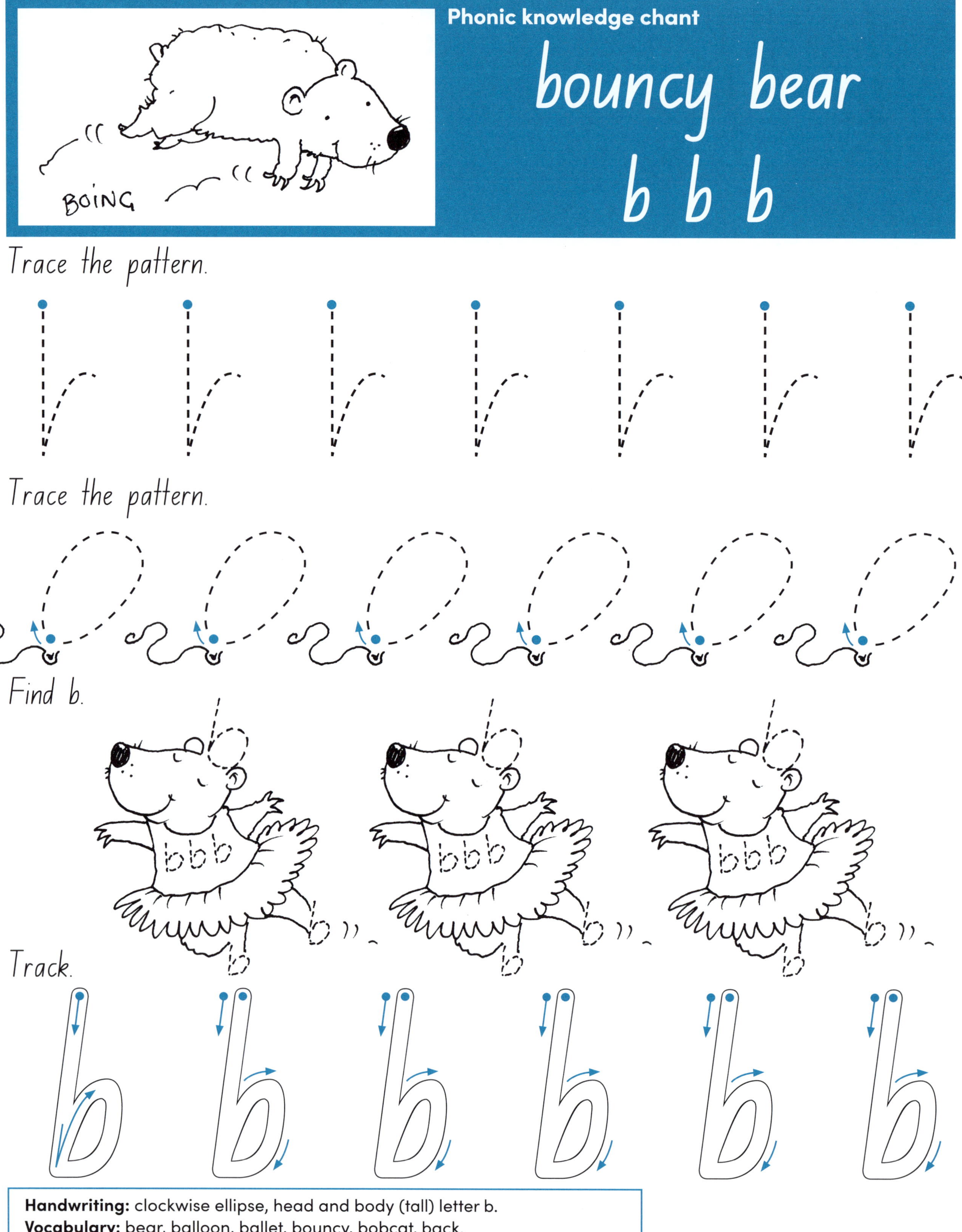

Handwriting: clockwise ellipse, head and body (tall) letter b.
Vocabulary: bear, balloon, ballet, bouncy, bobcat, back.
Phonic knowledge /b/: be, bee, by, bat, big, bit, bed, but, bug, bag, bad, bus.

Patter

Go down, come half way up, curve around and meet the downward diagonal stroke at the bottom. Keep your pencil on the page.

Phonic knowledge chant

pretty pig
p p p

Trace the pattern. Keep your pencil on the page.

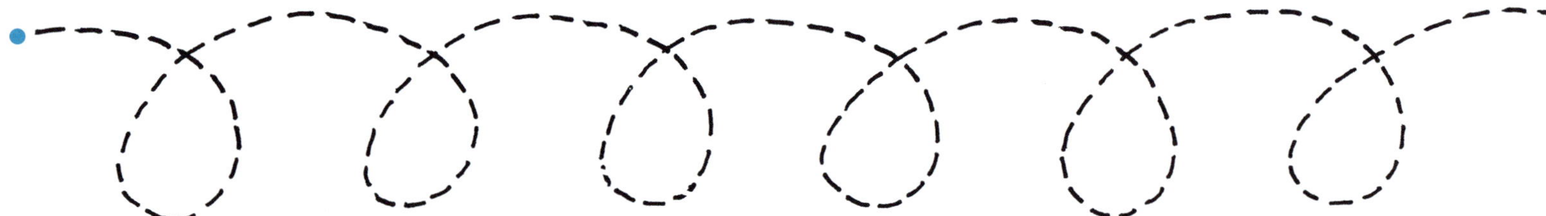

Trace the patterns.

Copy the pattern.

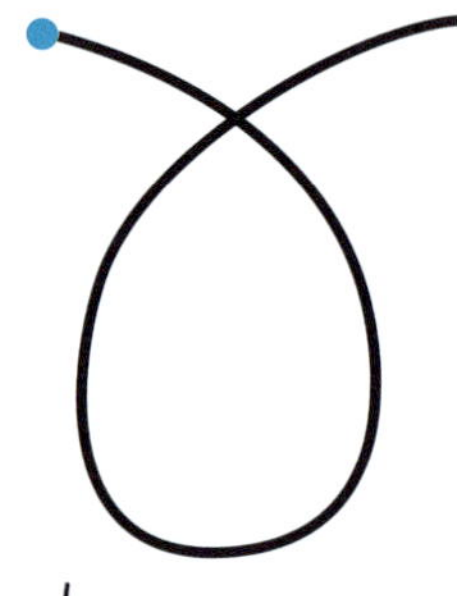

Track.

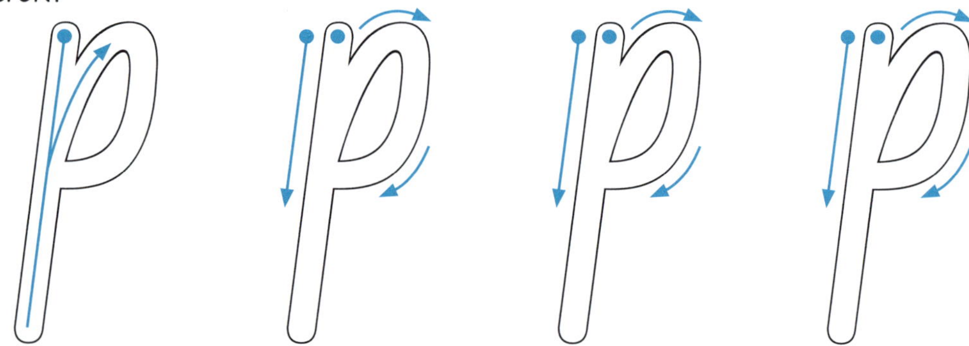

Handwriting: clockwise ellipse, body and tail (long) letter p.
Vocabulary: pretty, pink, prickly.
Phonic knowledge /p/: pig, pat, pit, pot, put, pan, pop, map, nip, top, tap.

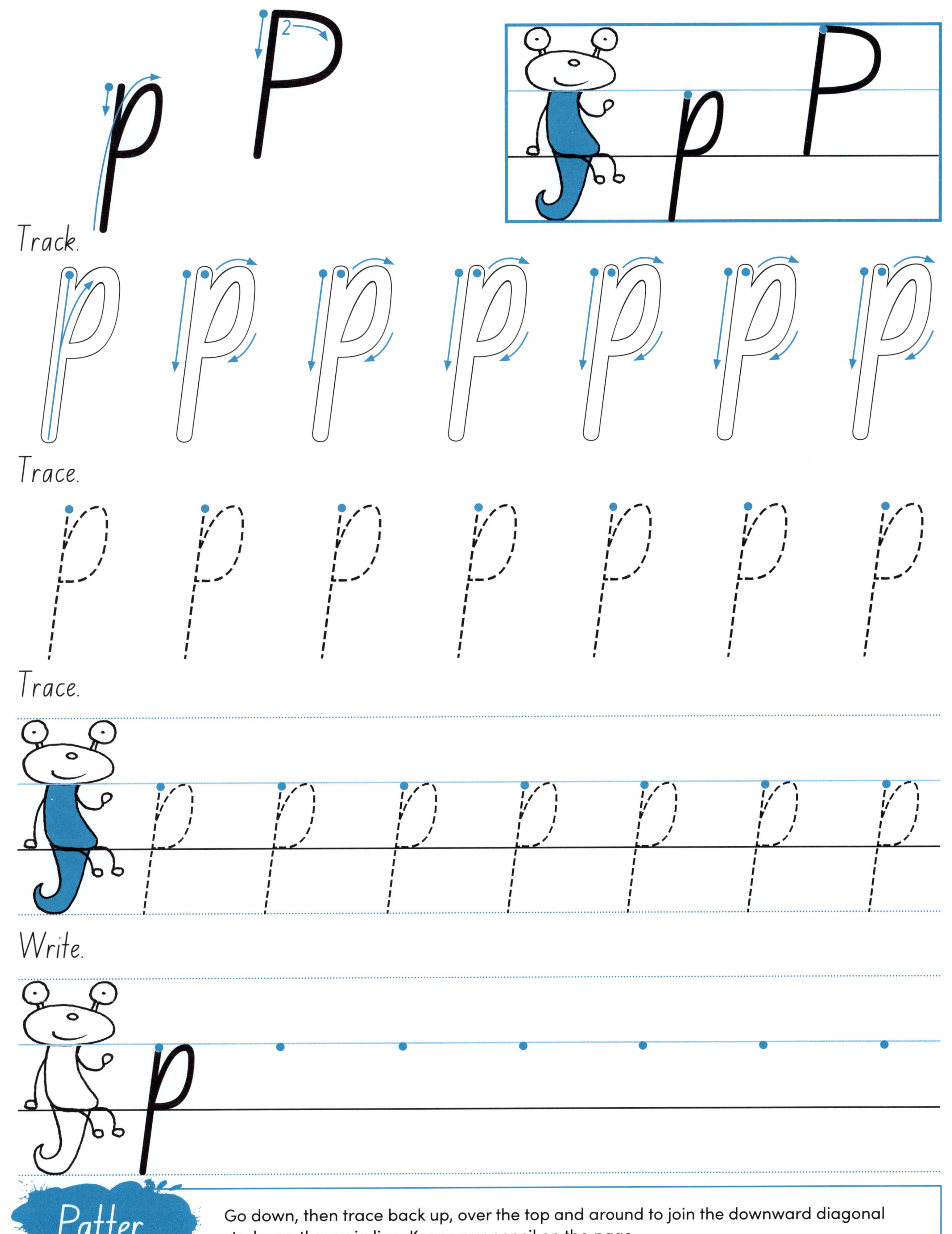

Patter

Go down, then trace back up, over the top and around to join the downward diagonal stroke on the main line. Keep your pencil on the page.

Phonic knowledge chant

lazy lion

l l l

Trace the pattern.

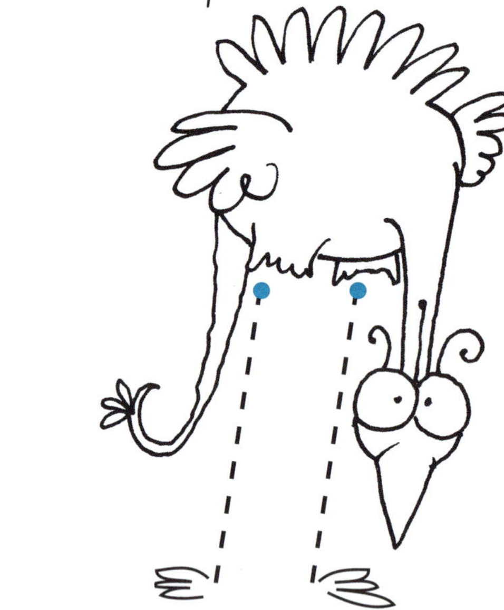

Trace the pattern.

Track.

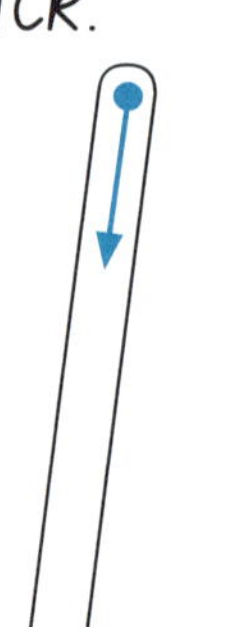

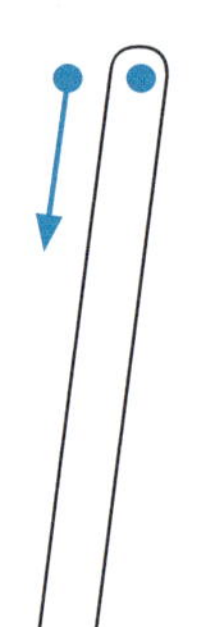

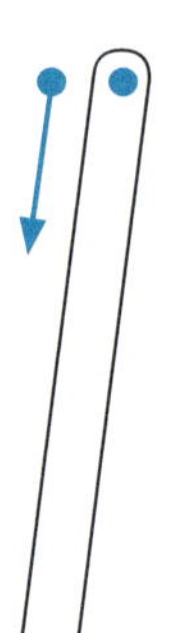

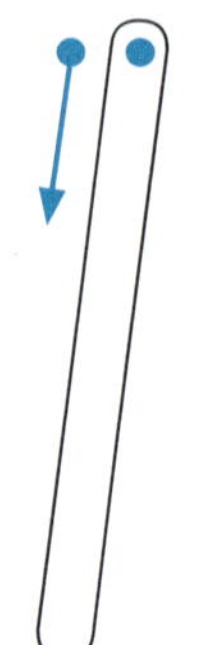

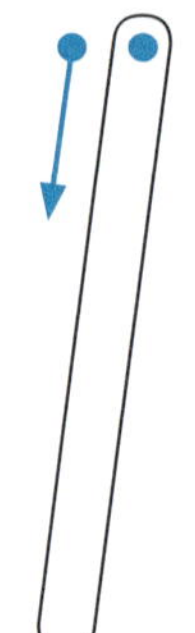

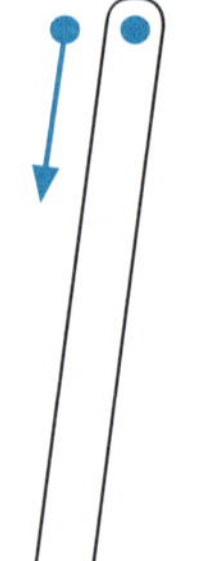

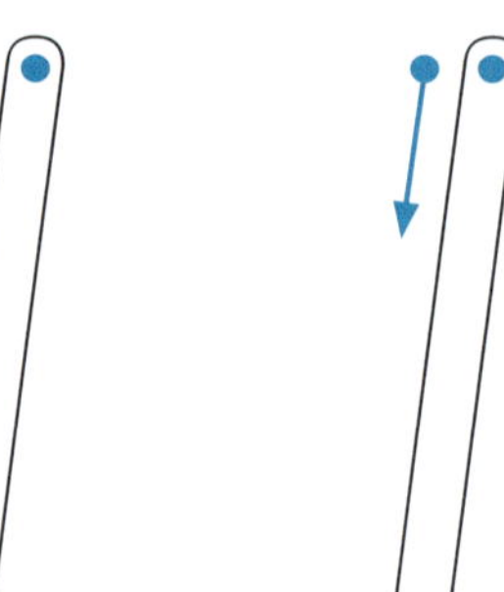

Handwriting: downward diagonal stroke, head and body (tall) letter l.
Vocabulary: lazy, lion, love, light, little, like, laptop.
Phonic knowledge /l/: lap, let, lot, lit, leg, land, lump, bell, fill, tell.

Start at the very top and draw a downward diagonal stroke that ends on the main line.

Phonic knowledge chant

tidy turtle

t t t

Trace the pattern.

Find t.

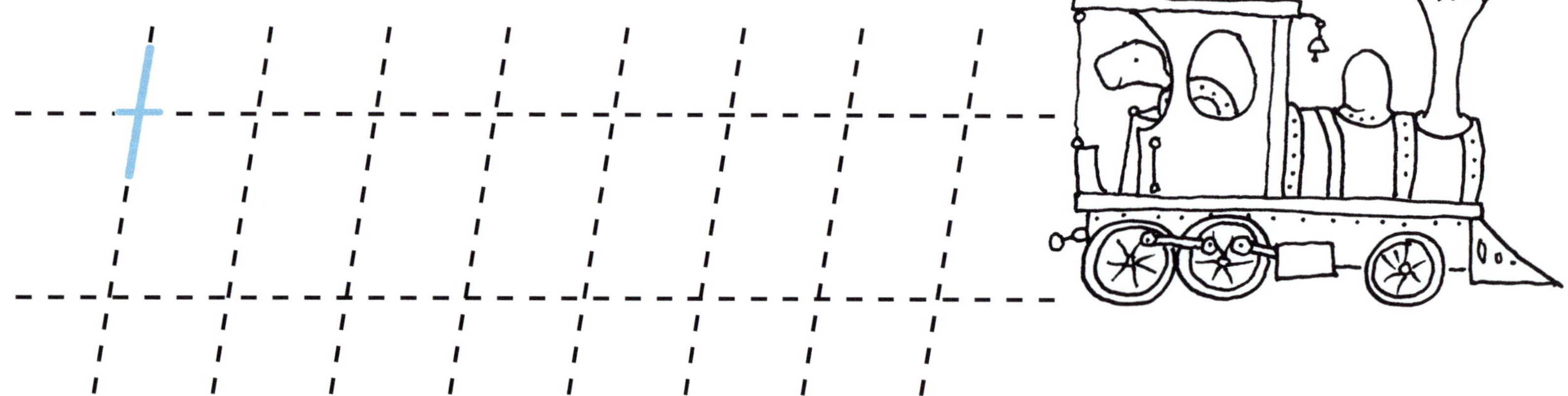

Track.

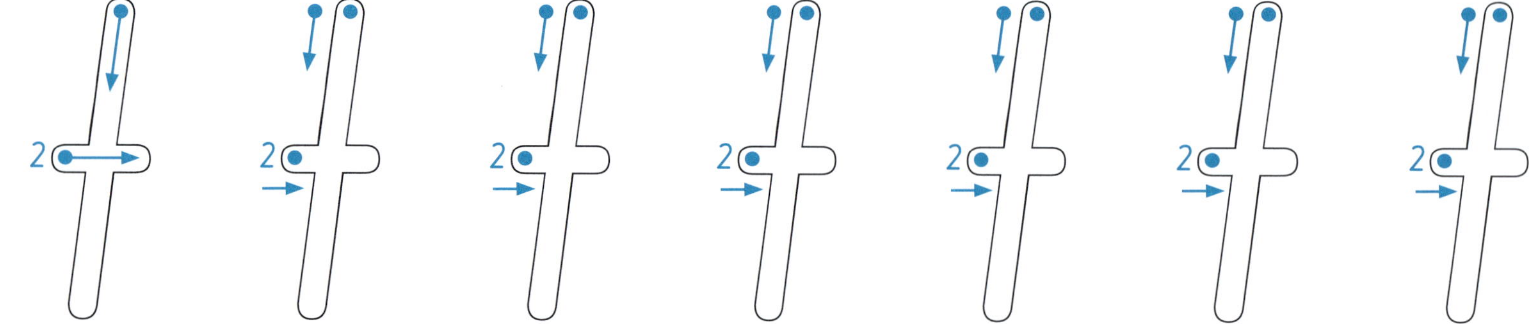

Handwriting: downward diagonal stroke, head and body (tall) letter t.
Vocabulary: tidy, turtle, track, train, tree, tortoise.
Phonic knowledge /t/: tap, tip, ten, it, sit, at, sat, pat, hot, get, pet, net.

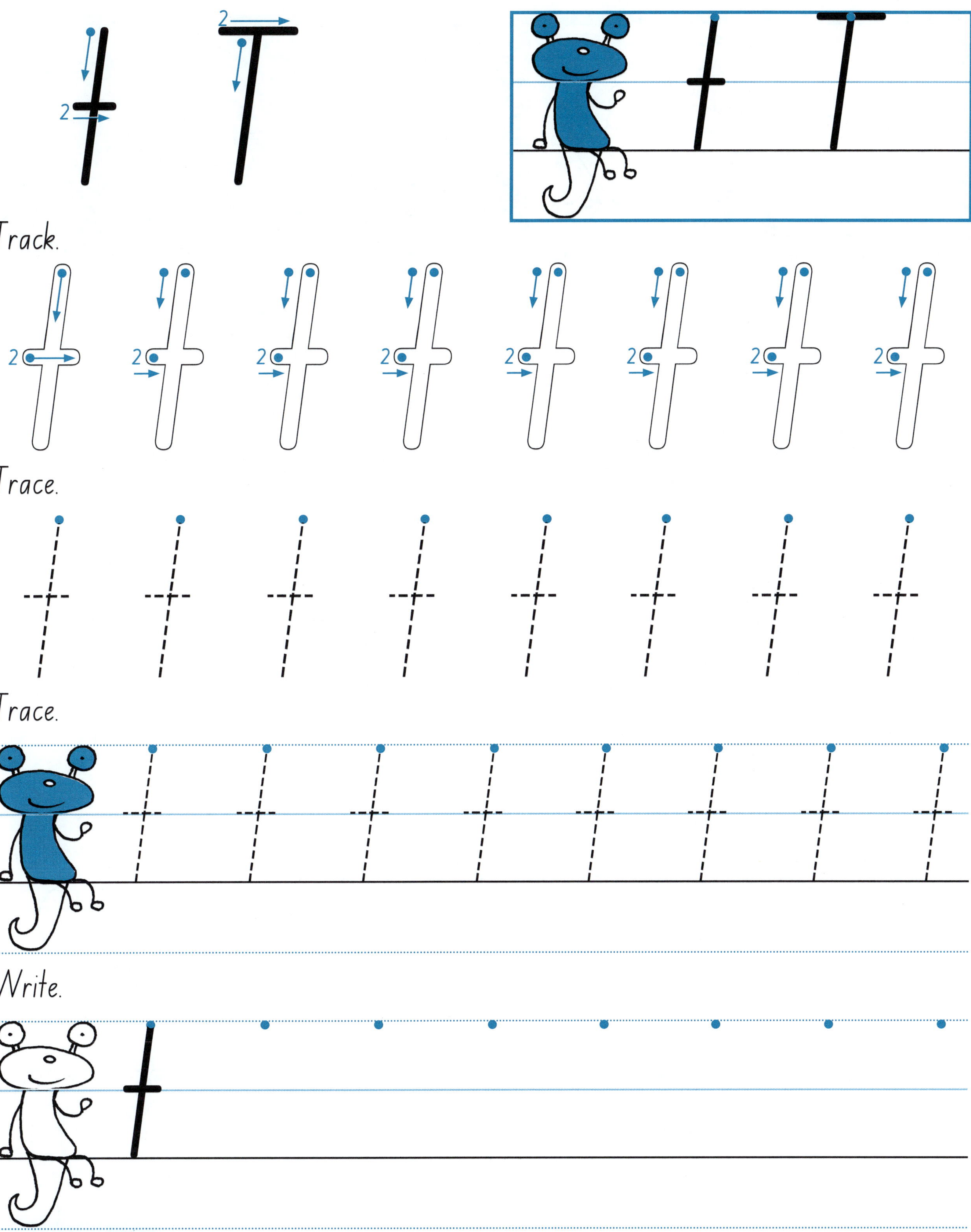

Patter

Start at the very top and draw a downward diagonal stroke that ends on the main line. Lift your pencil and make a cross.

Phonic knowledge chant

itchy iguana

i i i

Trace the pattern.

Trace.

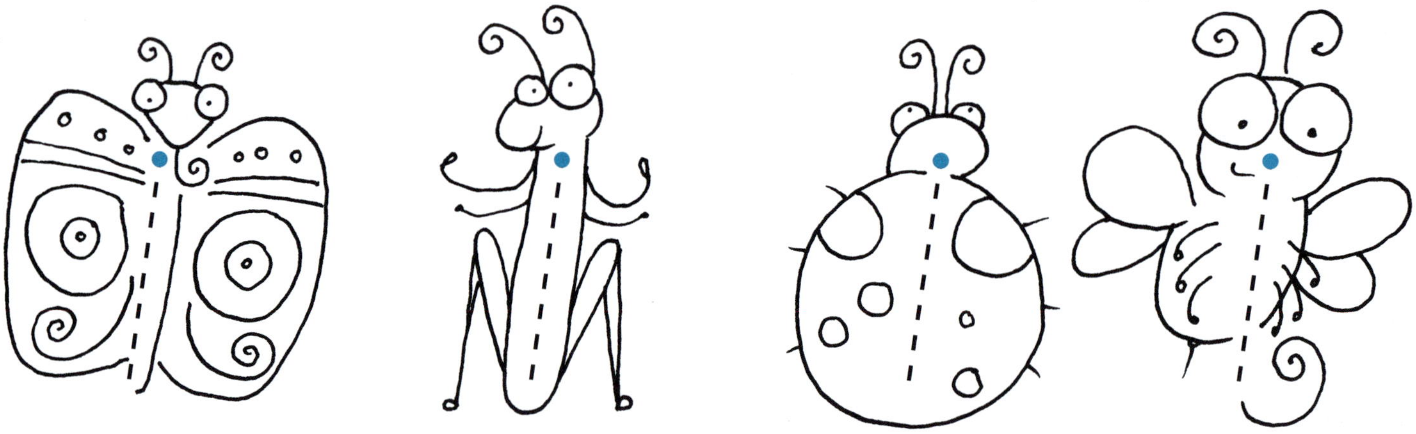

Trace.

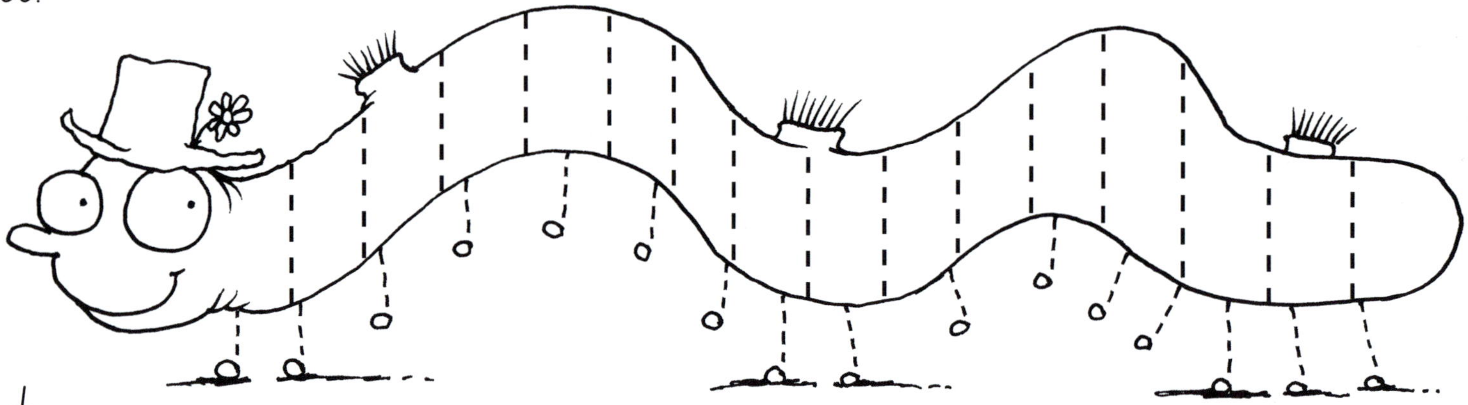

Track.

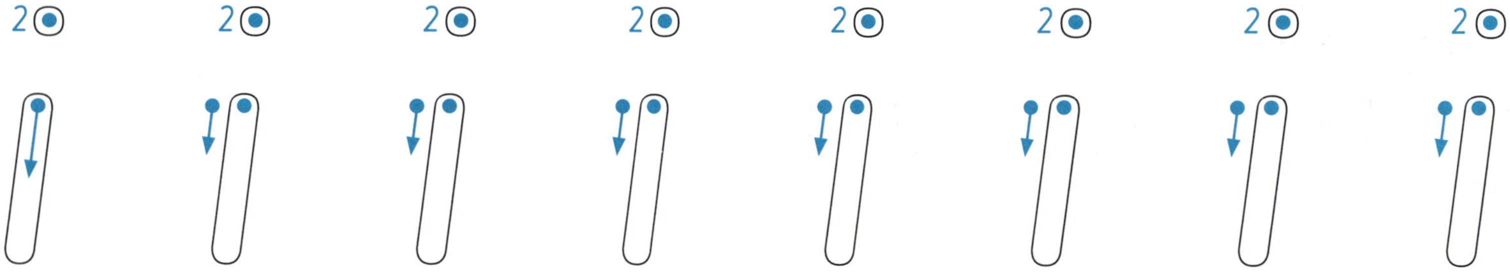

2 2 2 2 2 2 2 2

Handwriting: downward diagonal stroke, body (short) letter i.
Vocabulary: itchy, iguana, insect, will.
Phonic knowledge /i/: is, it, if, in, six, sit, lip, pit, tip.

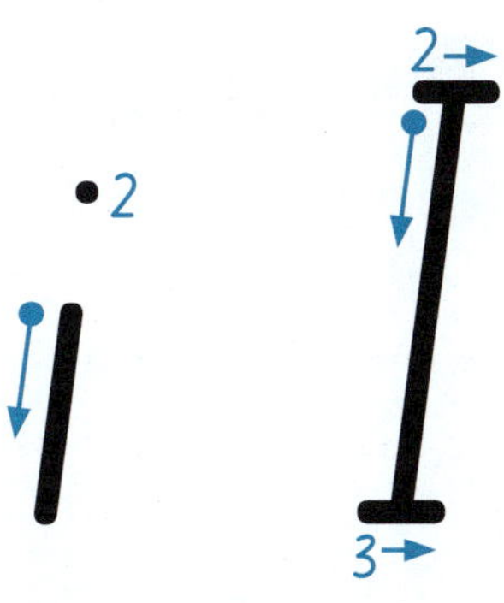

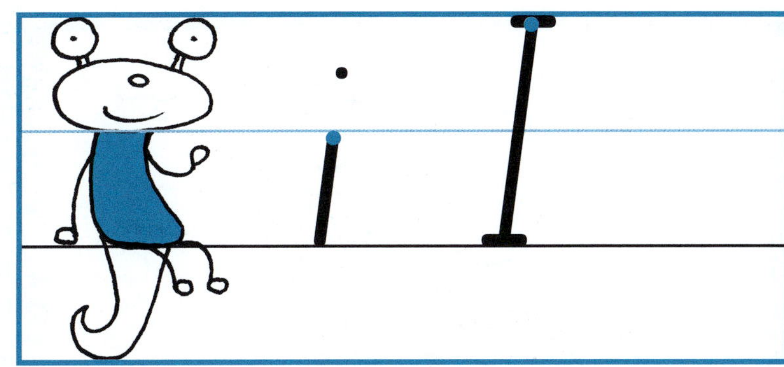

Trace the pattern. Keep your pencil on the page.

Copy the pattern.

illi

Trace.

Write.

i

Patter

Draw a downward diagonal stroke that ends on the main line. Lift your pencil and add a dot.

Phonic knowledge chant

jiggly jellyfish

j j j

Trace the pattern.

Trace the pattern. Keep your pencil on the page.

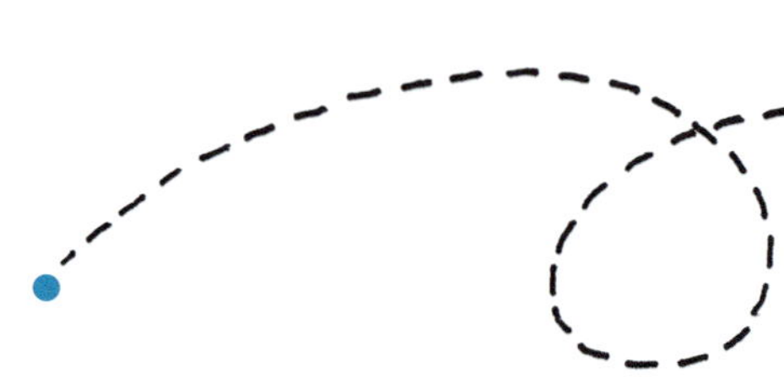 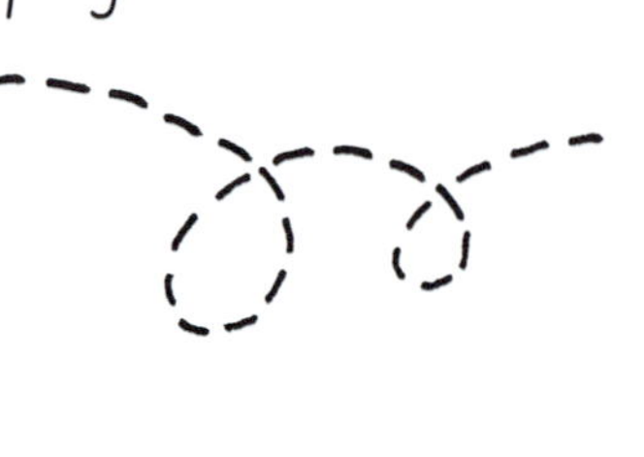 

Trace the pattern. Keep your pencil on the page.

 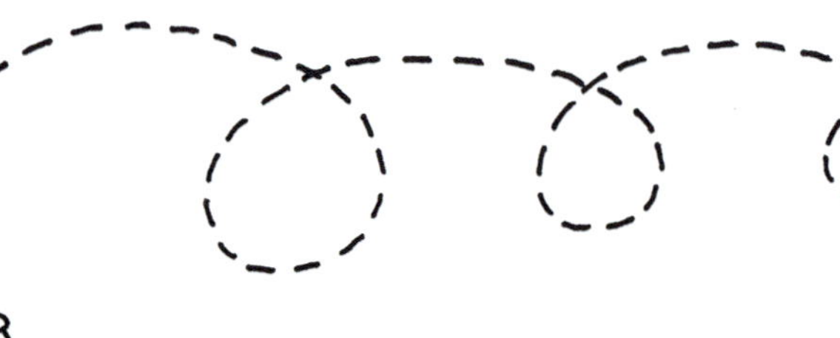 

Track.

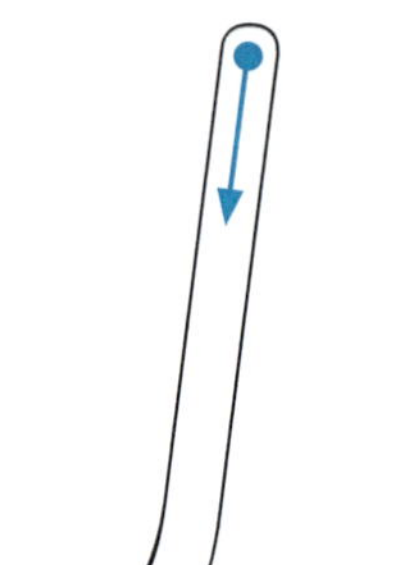 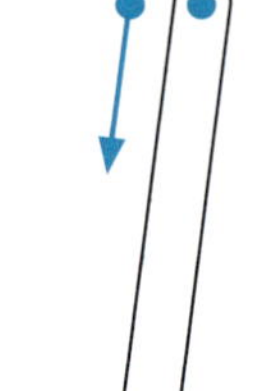 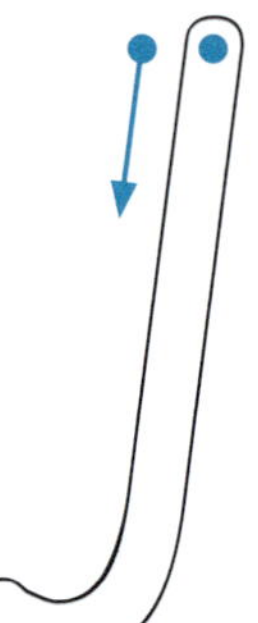 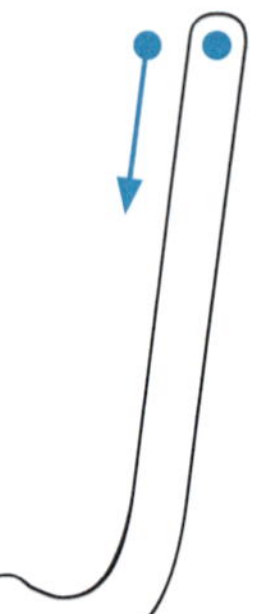 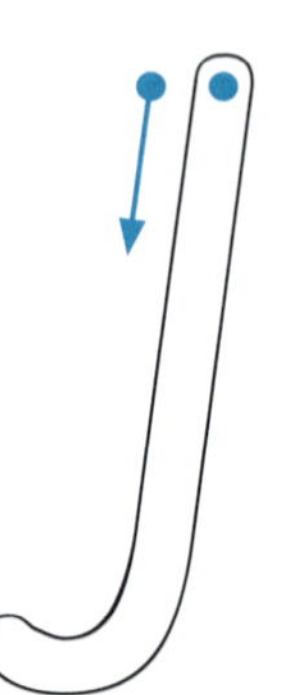  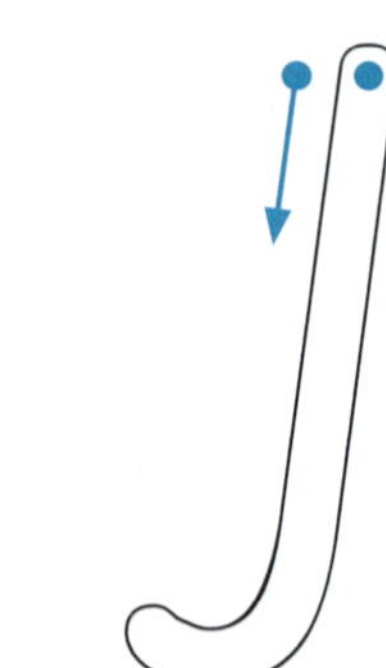

Handwriting: downward diagonal stroke, body and tail (long) letter j.
Vocabulary: jiggly, jellyfish, jump.
Phonic knowledge /j/: jam, job, jet, jog.

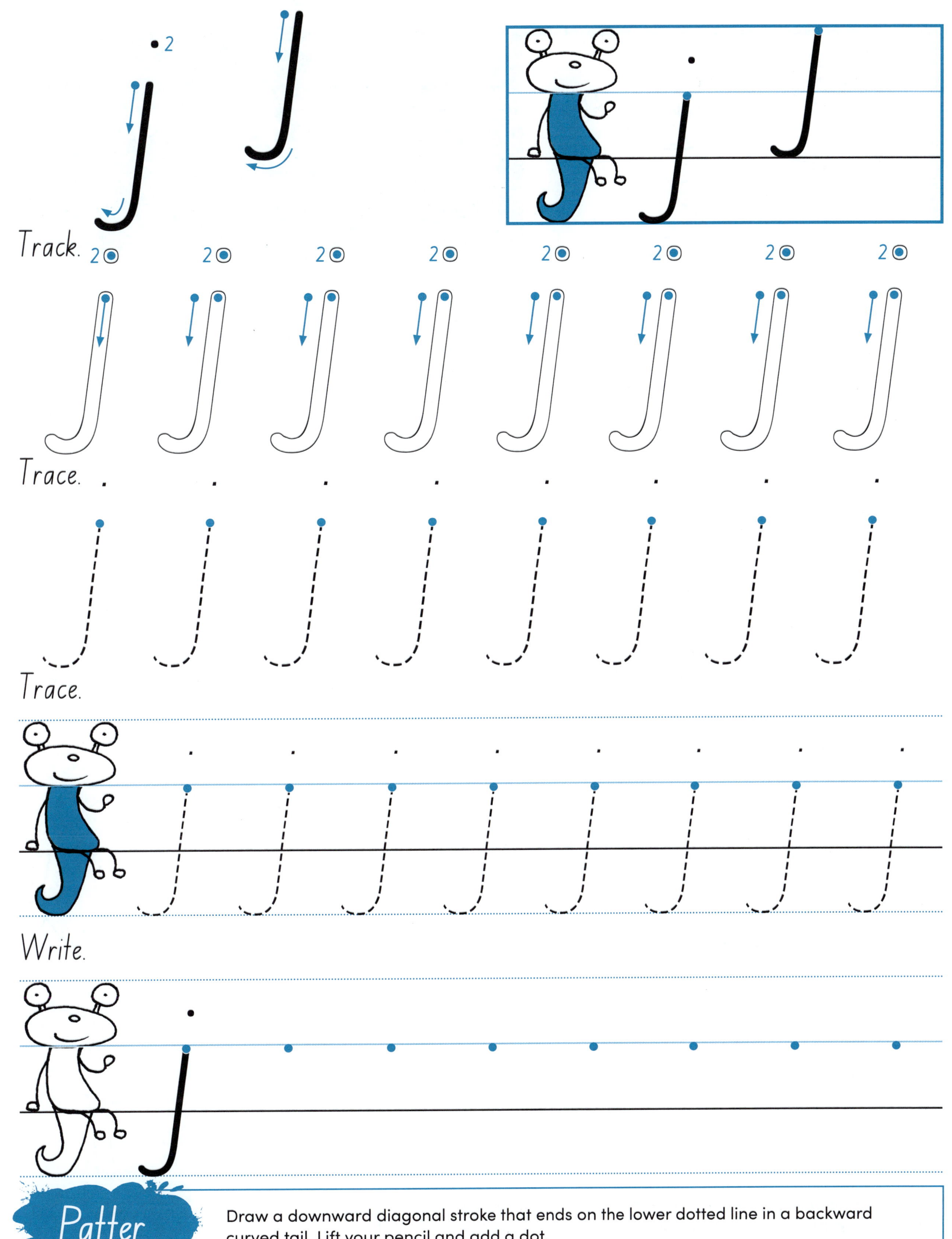
2
Track.
Trace.
Trace.
Write.
Patter
Draw a downward diagonal stroke that ends on the lower dotted line in a backward curved tail. Lift your pencil and add a dot.

Phonic knowledge chant

frisky frog
f f f

Trace the pattern.

Trace the pattern. Keep your pencil on the page.

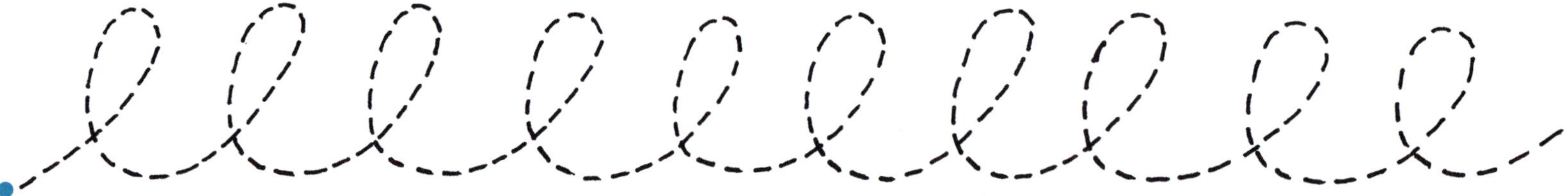

Find and write f.

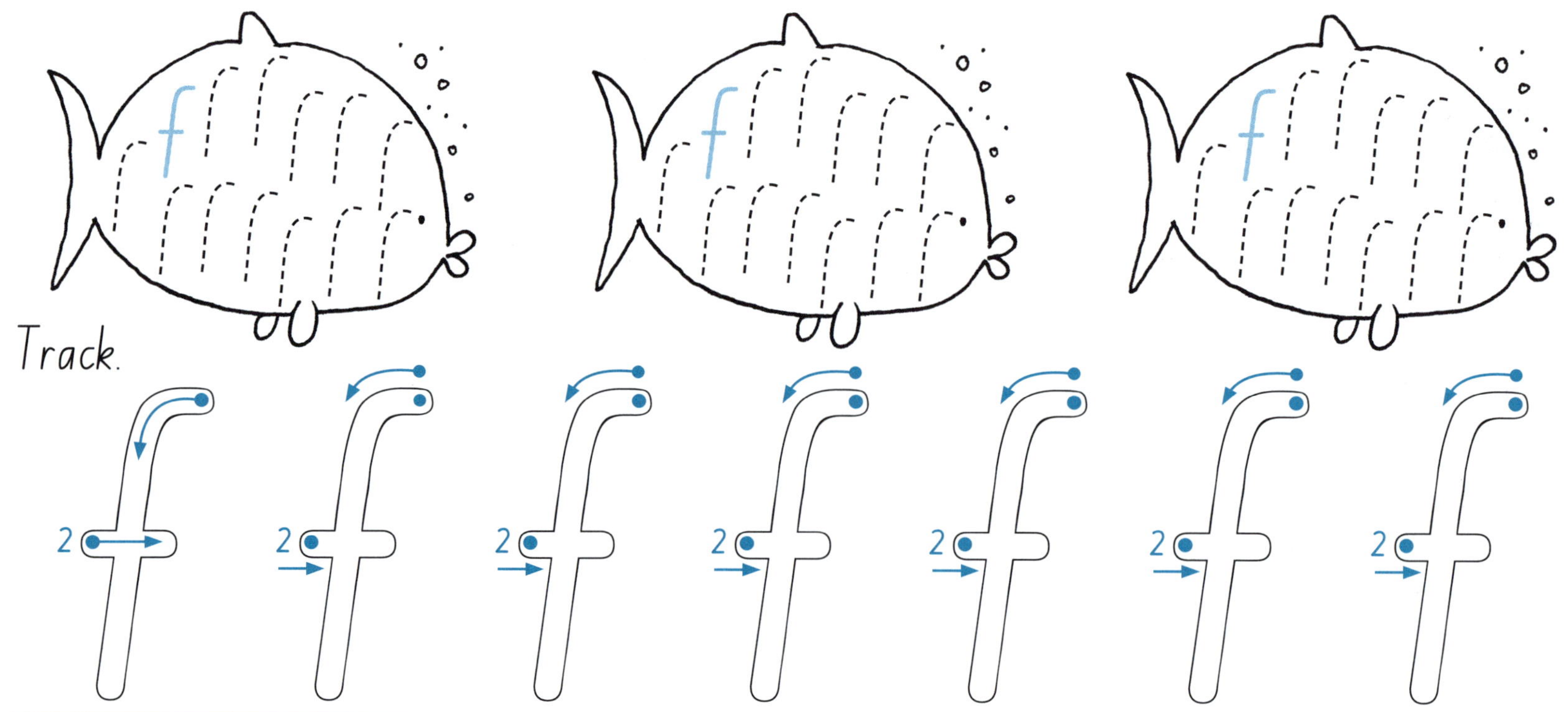

Handwriting: downward diagonal stroke, head and body (tall) letter f.
Vocabulary: frisky, frog, fish, flower.
Phonic knowledge /f/: fun, fin, fan, fit, fat, fog, if, puff, huff, cuff.

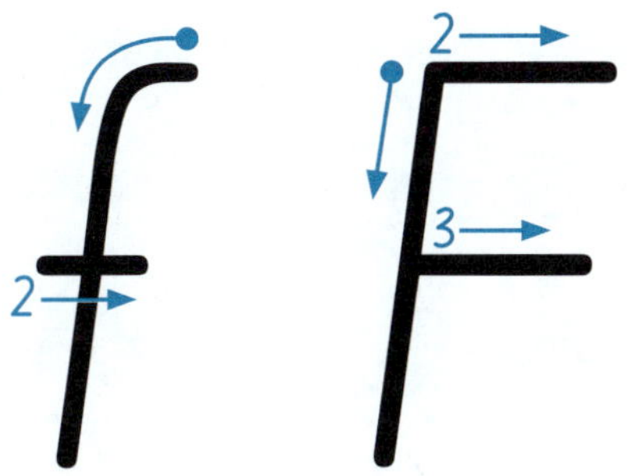

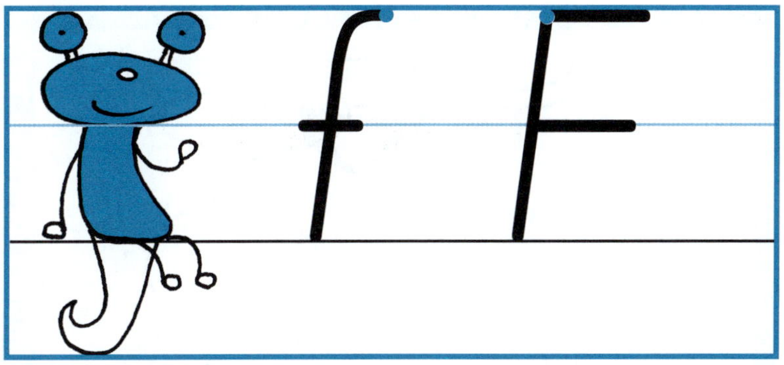

f F

Track.

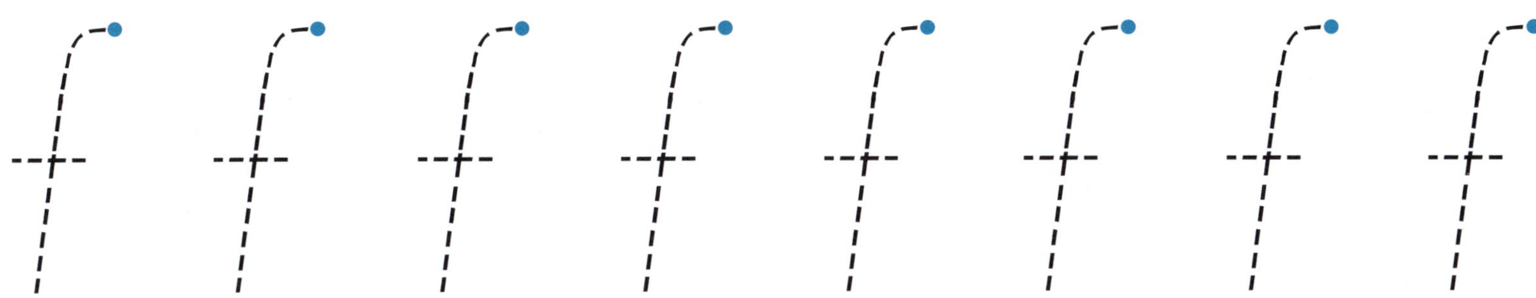

Trace.

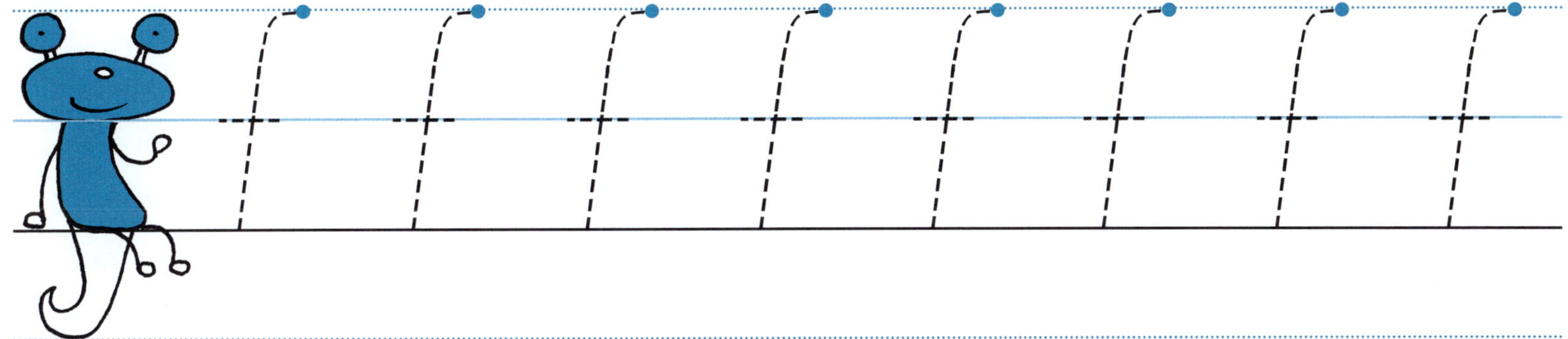

Trace.

Write.

Patter

Go backwards in a curve and then make a diagonal downstroke to the main line. Lift your pencil and make a cross.

Phonic knowledge chant

foxy ox

x x x

Track the pattern.

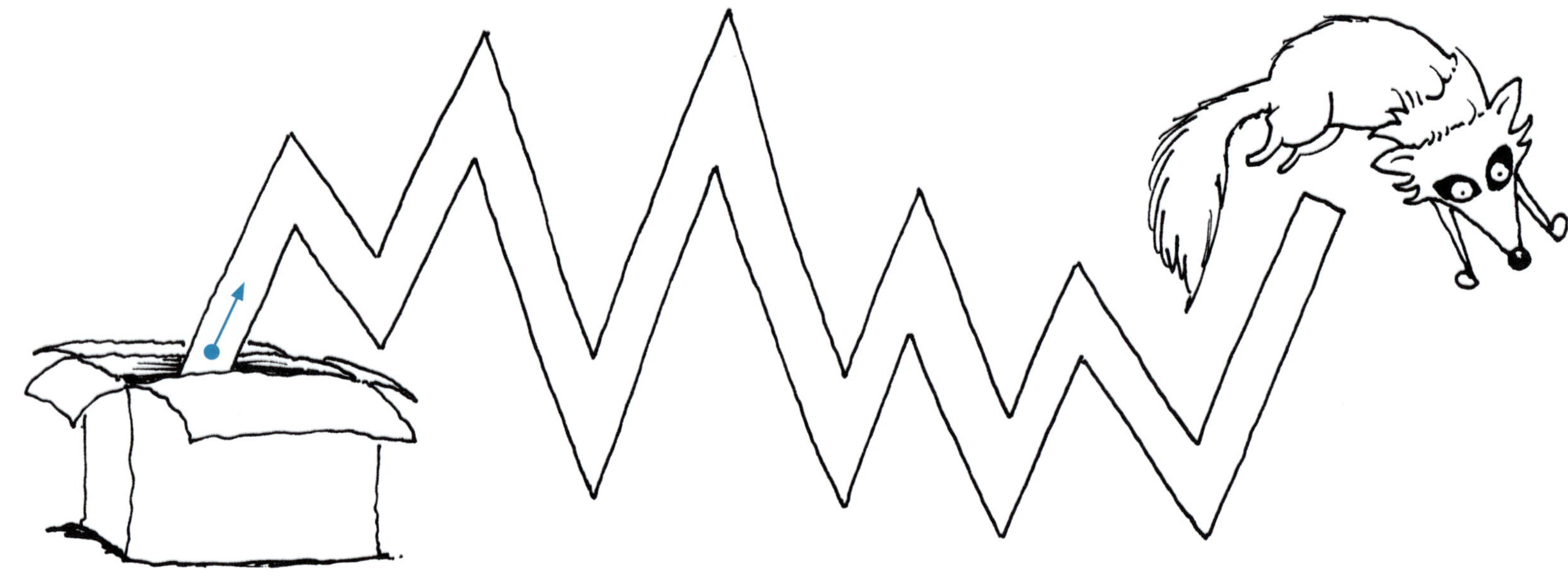

Trace the pattern. Find and write x.

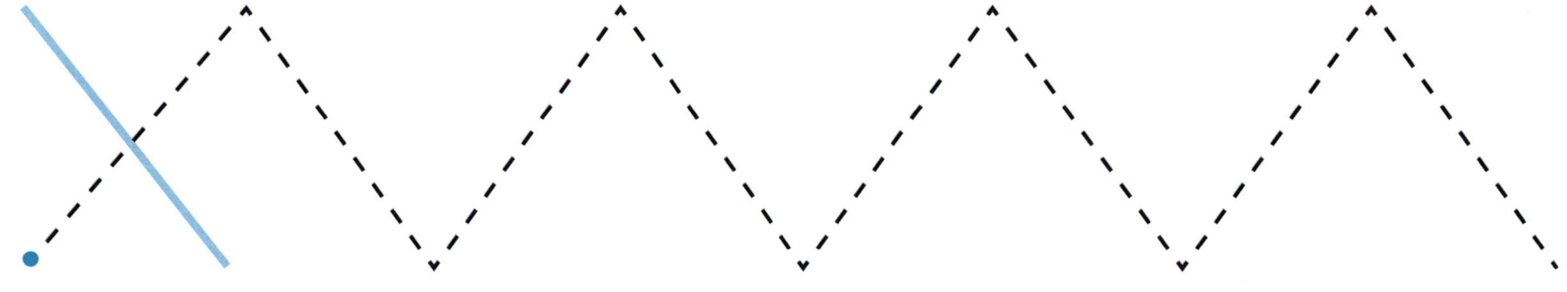

Track.

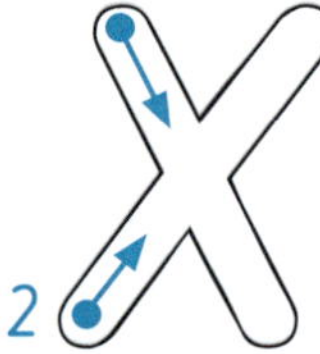
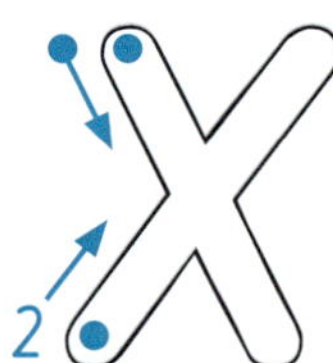
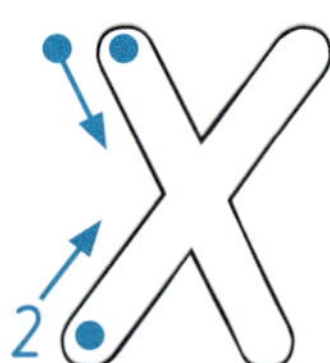
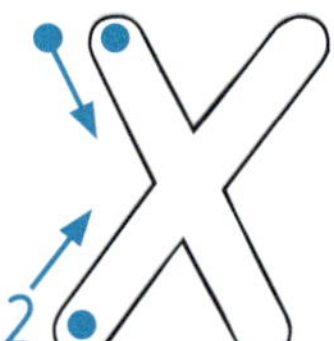
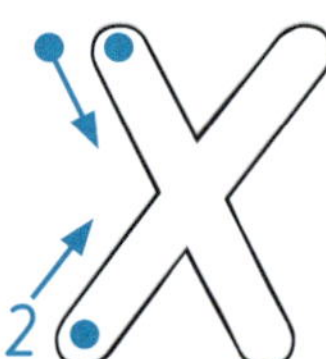
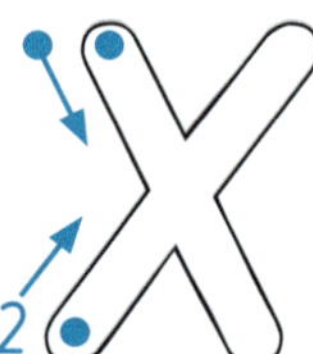

Handwriting: downward diagonal stroke, body (short) letter x.
Vocabulary: X-ray.
Phonic knowledge /ks/: mix, fix, box, six, fox, ox.

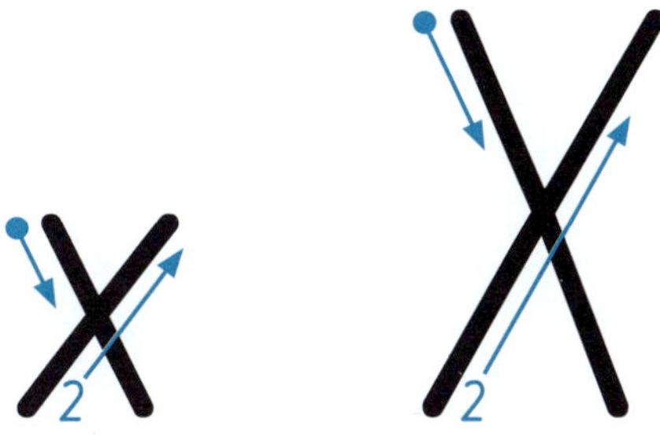
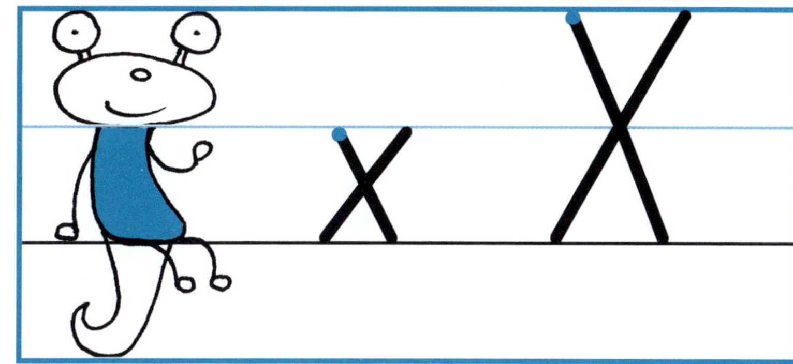

Track.

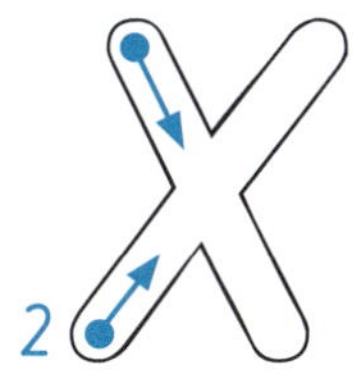 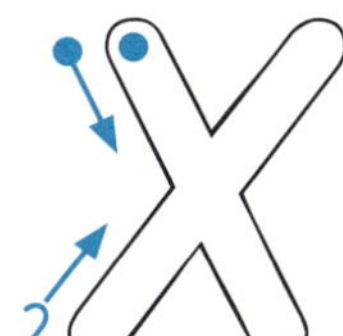 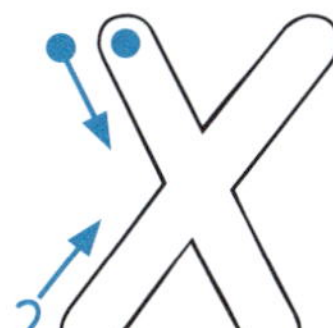 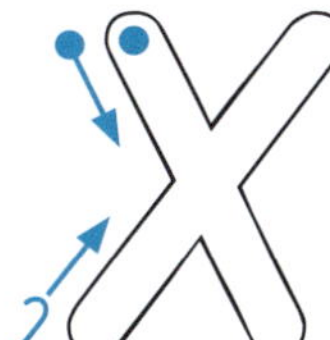 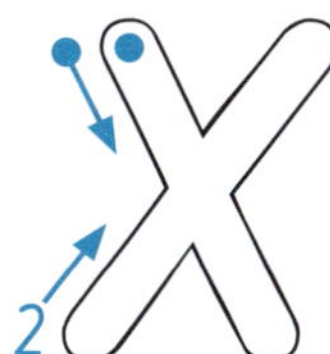 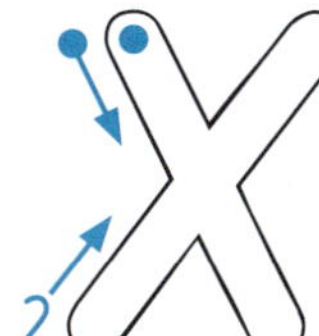 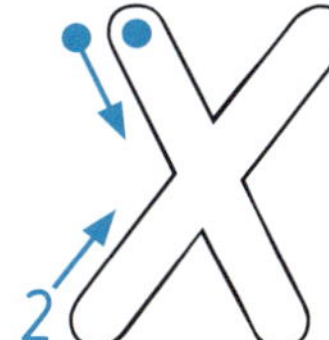

Trace.

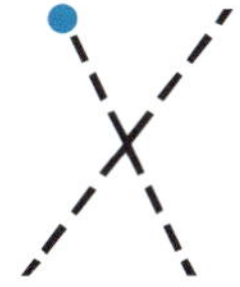  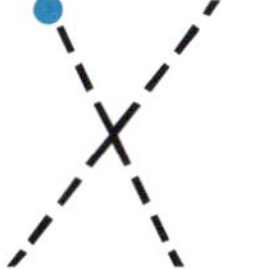    

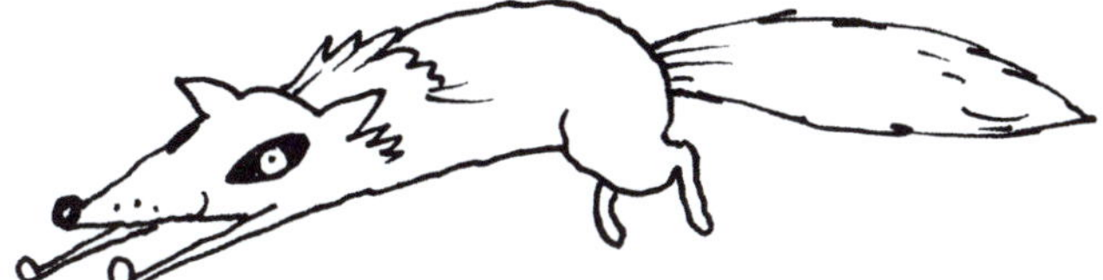

Trace.

 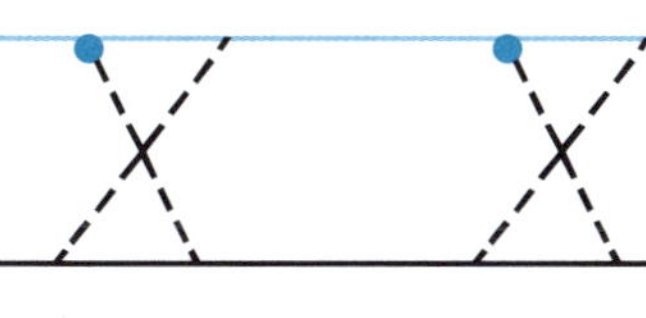 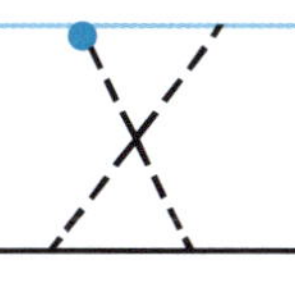 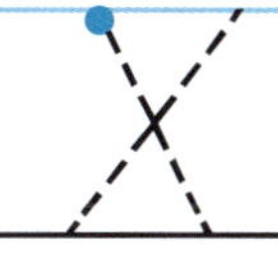 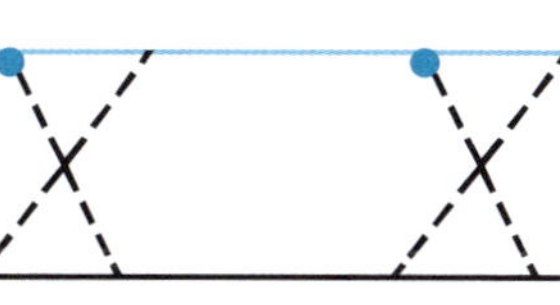

Write.

Make a sloping downstroke. Lift your pencil and go up to cross it with another line.

Phonic knowledge chant

zigzag zebra

z z z

Trace the pattern.

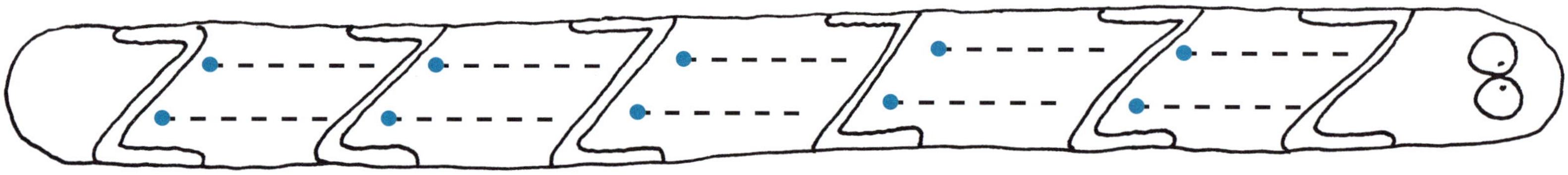

Trace the pattern.

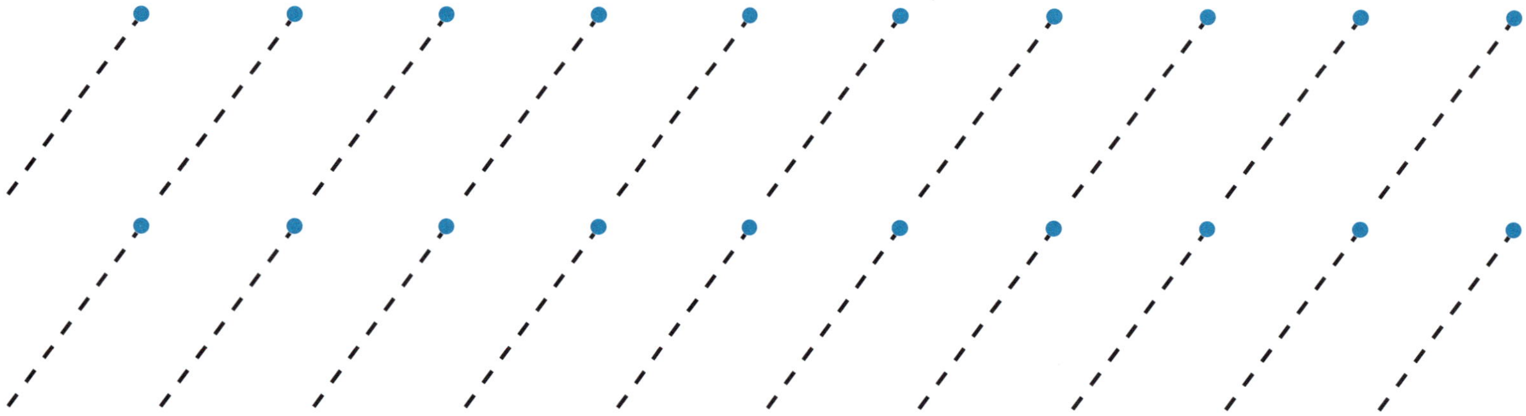

Find z.

Track.

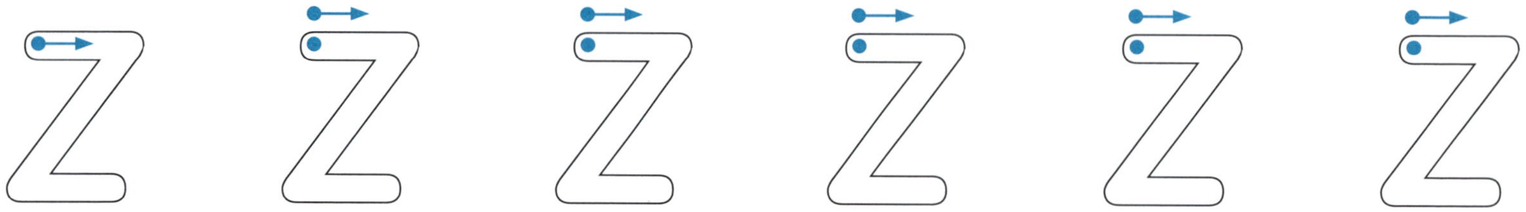

Handwriting: downward diagonal stroke, body (short) letter z.
Vocabulary: zigzag, zebra, zoo, pizza, zipper.
Phonic knowledge /z/: zip, zap, buzz, jazz, fizz.

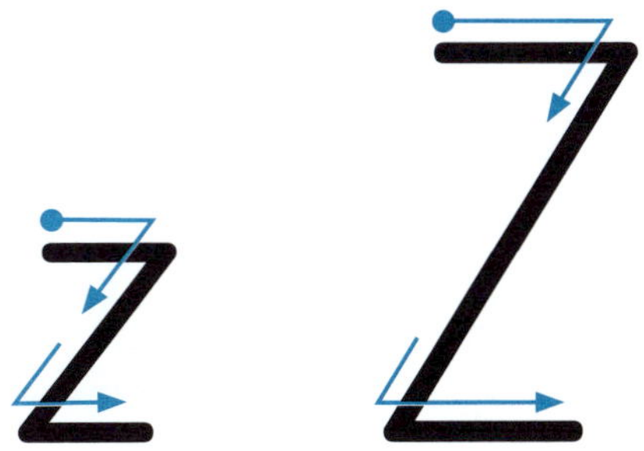

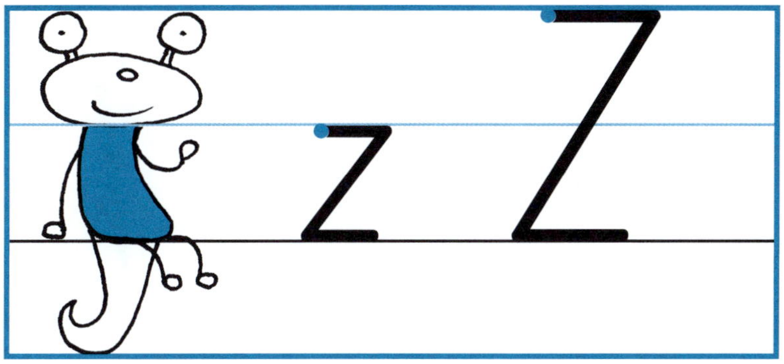

z Z

z Z

Track.

Trace.

Trace.

Write.

z

Patter

Go straight across, then make a sloping backwards line to the main line, and then go straight across again. Keep your pencil on the page.

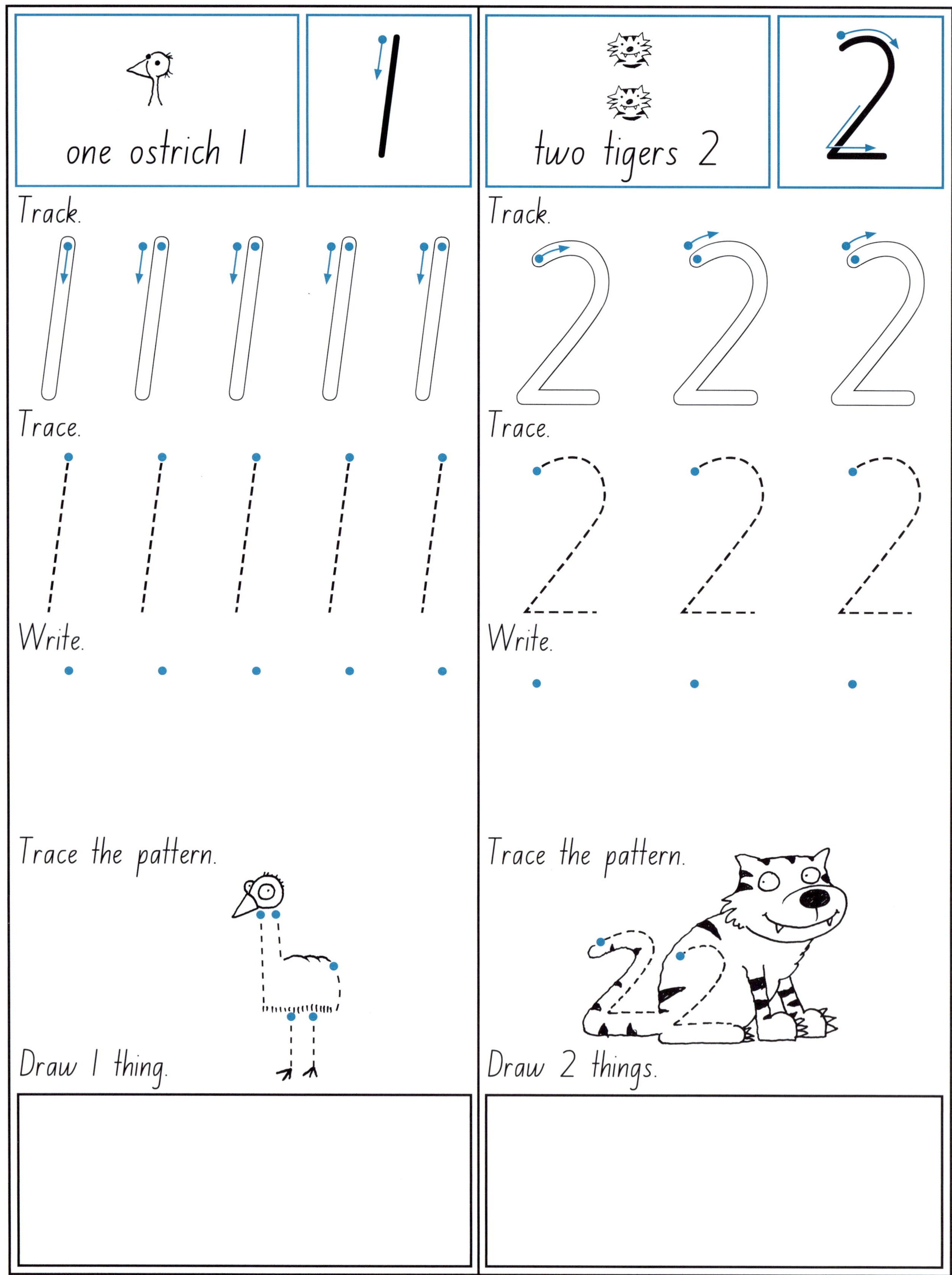
one ostrich 1
1
two tigers 2
2
Track.
Trace.
Write.
Trace the pattern.
Draw 1 thing.
Track.
Trace.
Write.
Trace the pattern.
Draw 2 things.

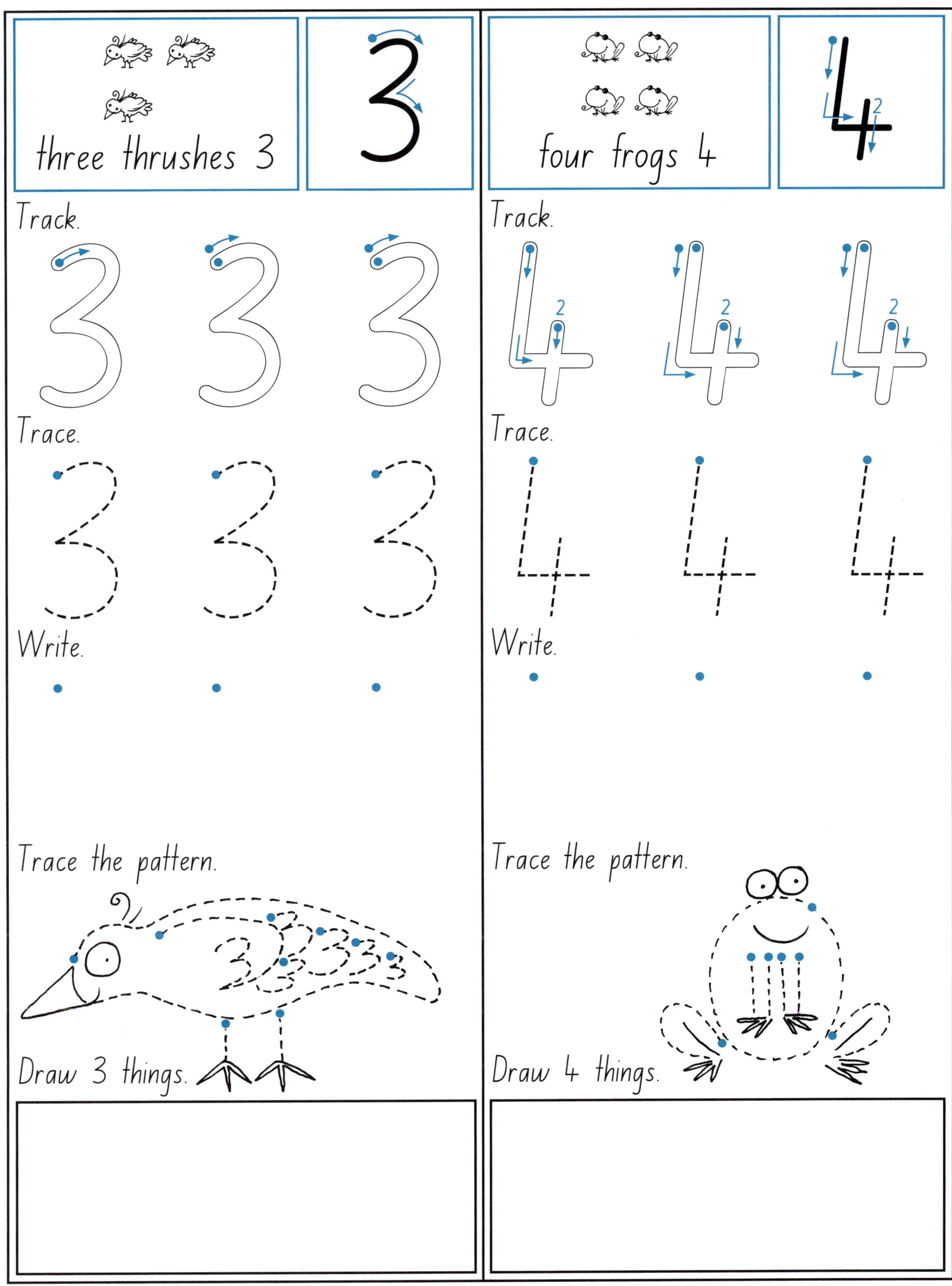
three thrushes 3
3
Track.
Trace.
Write.
Trace the pattern.
Draw 3 things.
four frogs 4
4
2
Track.
Trace.
Write.
Trace the pattern.
Draw 4 things.

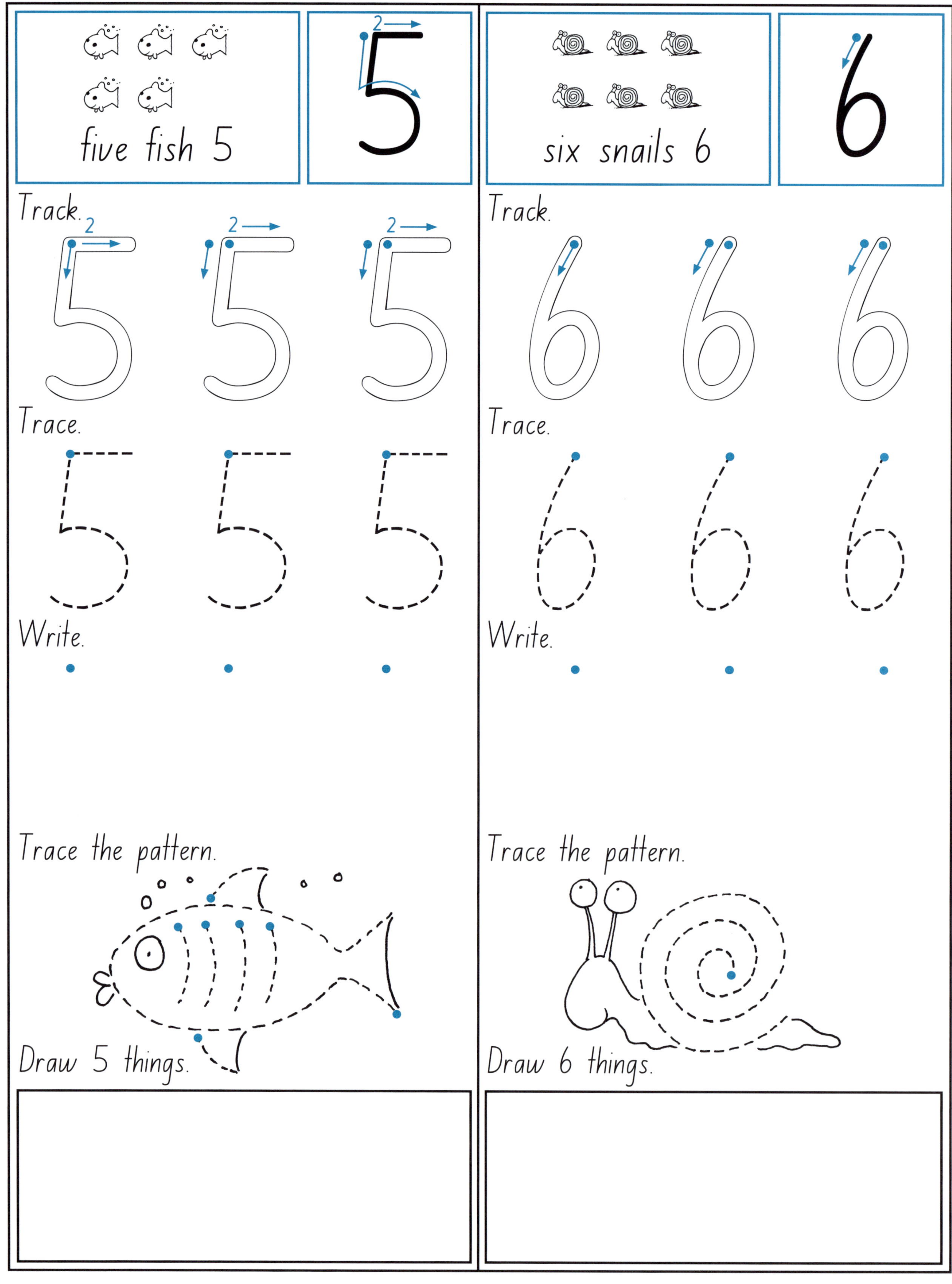
five fish 5
Track.
Trace.
Write.
Trace the pattern.
Draw 5 things.
six snails 6
Track.
Trace.
Write.
Trace the pattern.
Draw 6 things.

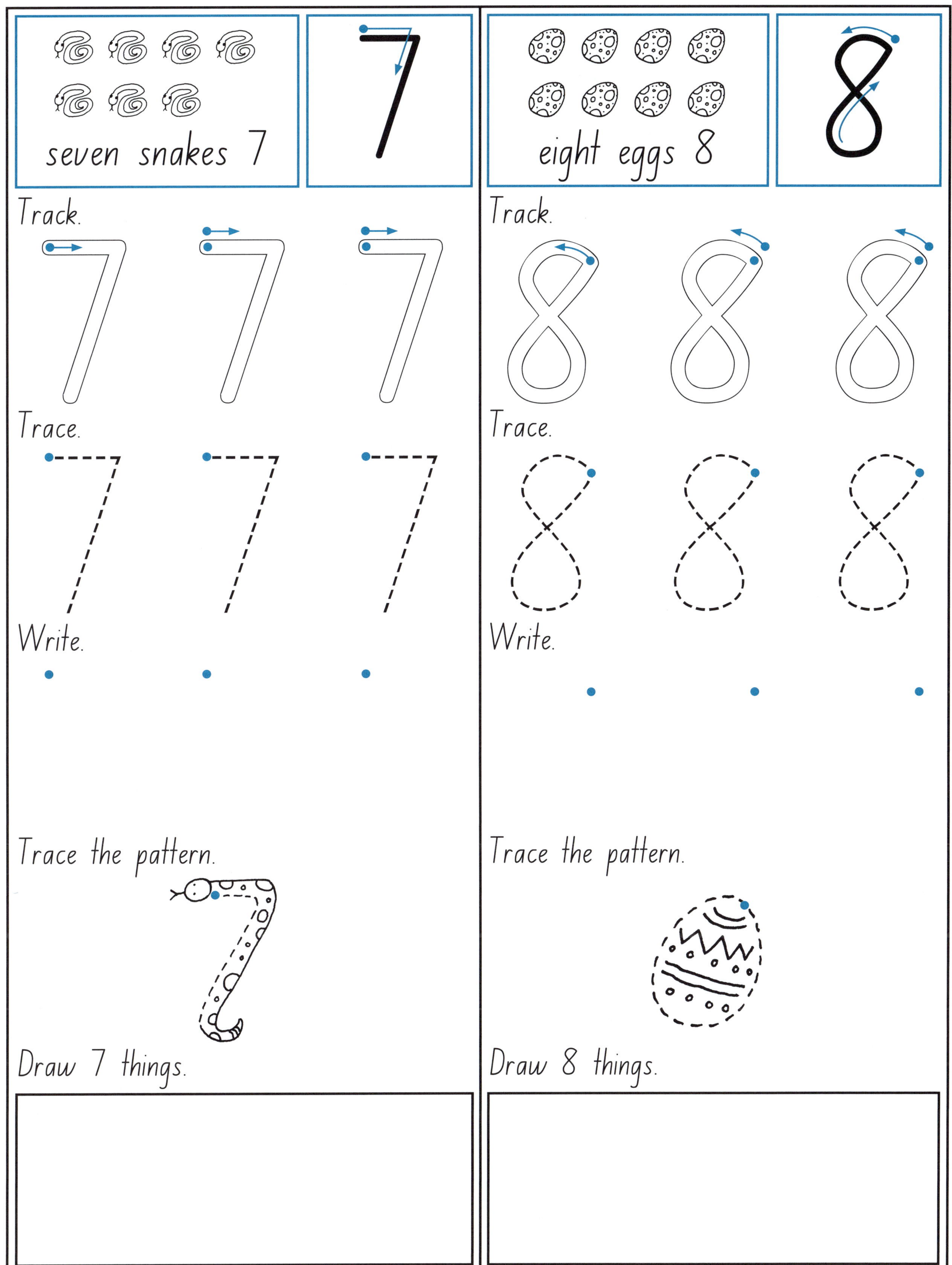
seven snakes 7
Track.
Trace.
Write.
Trace the pattern.
Draw 7 things.
eight eggs 8
Track.
Trace.
Write.
Trace the pattern.
Draw 8 things.

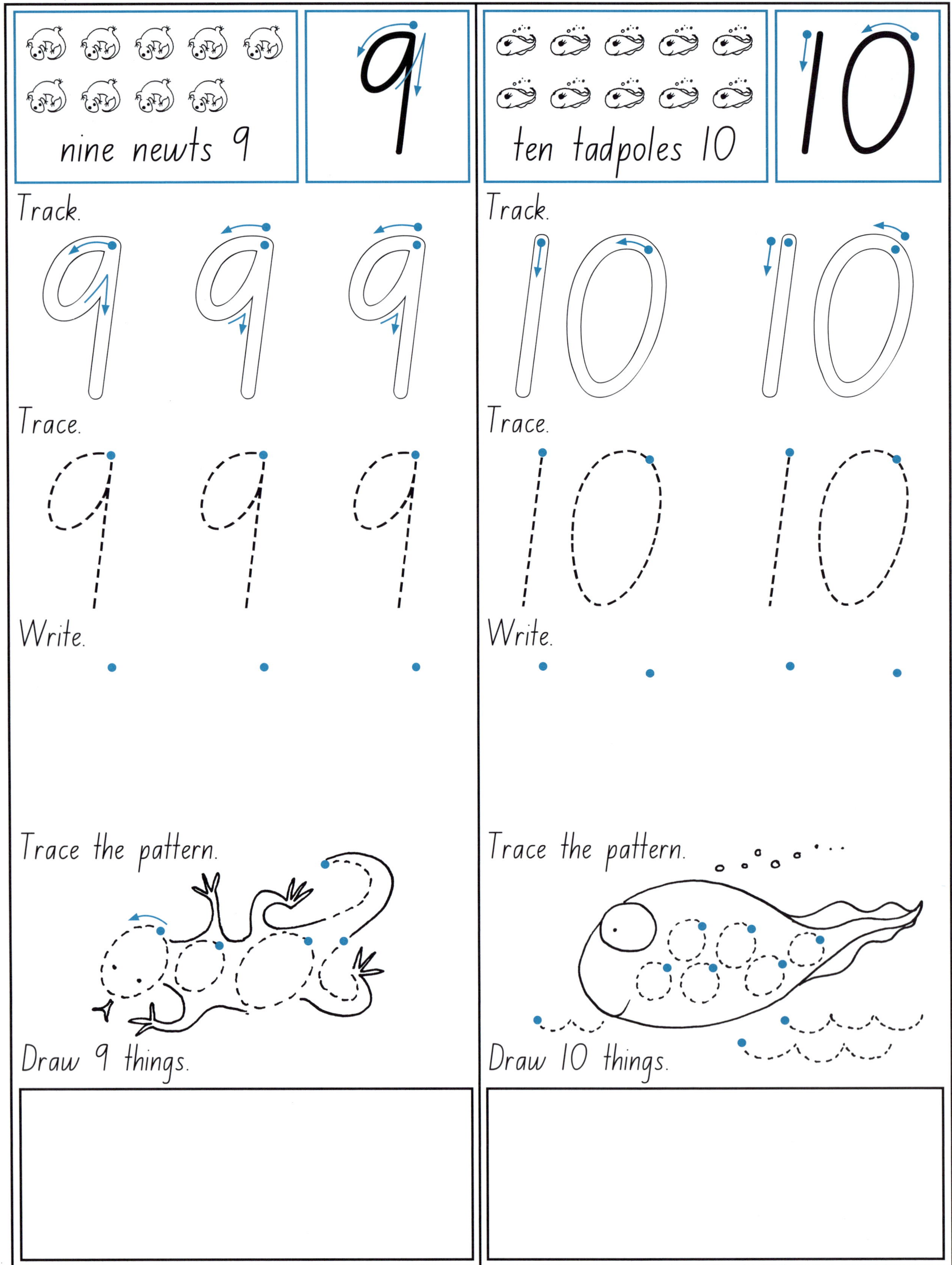
nine newts 9
9
ten tadpoles 10
10
Track.
Track.
Trace.
Trace.
Write.
Write.
Trace the pattern.
Trace the pattern.
Draw 9 things.
Draw 10 things.